ETERNAL
SEASONS

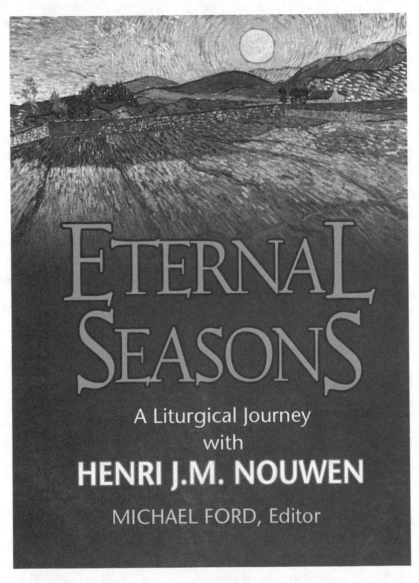

ETERNAL
SEASONS

A Liturgical Journey
with
HENRI J.M. NOUWEN

MICHAEL FORD, Editor

 SORIN BOOKS   Notre Dame, Indiana

Excerpts from *The New Jerusalem Bible*, copyright © 1985 by Darton, Longman & Todd, Ltd., and Doubleday, a division of Bantam Doubleday Dell Publishing Group, Inc. Used with permission of the publisher.

www.sorinbooks.com

International Standard Book Number: 1-893732-77-0

Cover and text design by John Carson
Cover art: Landscape with Rising Sun by Vincent van Gogh 1889 ©Corbis.
All Rights Reserved.

Printed and bound in the United States of America.

Library of Congress Cataloging-in-Publication Data
Ford, Michael, 1956-
  Eternal seasons : a liturgical journey with Henri J.M. Nouwen / Michael Ford.
    p.
  Originally published: London : Darton, Longman and Todd, 2003.
  Includes bibliographical references.
  ISBN 1-893732-77-0
  1. Nouwen, Henri J. M. 2. Catholic Church--Liturgy. 3. Church year.
  I. Title.
  BX1970 .F66 2004
  242'.3--dc22

                                                              2003021463

We forget sacred time in our preoccupation
with the illusion of linear time.
　　—*Maggie Ross*

*This book is dedicated to Father John Squire
and all friends at St. Andrew's Church, Taunton, England,
where I first experienced the richness of the
liturgical year close to the beauty of the
Somerset countryside.*

Contents

Acknowledgments

I am indebted to Father John and Mrs. Ruth Squire, and to my friends at St. Andrew's Church, Taunton, England, for their loyalty and spiritual companionship over so many years. My thanks also to the current parish priest, the Reverend Julian Smith, who is always welcoming and supportive; to Canon Peter Huxham for our celebrations of the "Christmas Triduum" in the hospital chapel of Musgrove Park; to Dr David Torevell, author of *Losing the Sacred*, for our liturgical conversations over two decades; to Ken Bird, editor-in-chief of the *Somerset County Gazette*, for his friendship and professional support; and in North America to Sue Mosteller C.S.J., literary executrix, estate of Henri J.M. Nouwen, Maureen Wright, administrator, Henri Nouwen Literary Centre, Gabrielle Earnshaw, archivist, The Henri J.M. Nouwen Archives and Research Collection, and Robert Durback, for their interest and kindness.

I should like to acknowledge warmly my publishers, Darton, Longman and Todd Ltd, in particular my editor, Virginia Hearn, for her unfailing professionalism, personal encouragement and creative spirit. My appreciation at DLT is extended to Rachel

Davis, Kathy Dyke Eleanor Fletcher, Leslie Kay, Helen Porter and Brendan Walsh.

To my family and close friends, my continuing gratitude.

Jesus and Mary: Finding Our Sacred Center © 1993 by Henri J.M. Nouwen. Used with permission of the publisher, St. Anthony Messenger Press, 28 W. Liberty St., Cincinnati, OH 45202, USA.

The Genesee Diary by Henri J.M. Nouwen, © 1976 by Henri J.M. Nouwen. Used by permission of Doubleday, a division of Random House, Inc. Also published by Darton, Longman and Todd in the United Kingdom.

A Cry for Mercy by Henri J.M. Nouwen, © 1981 by Henri J.M. Nouwen. Used by permission of Doubleday, a division of Random House, Inc.

The Road to Daybreak by Henri J.M. Nouwen, © 1988 by Henri J.M. Nouwen. Used by permission of Doubleday, a division of Random House, Inc. Also published by Darton, Longman and Todd in the United Kingdom.

Lifesigns by Henri J.M. Nouwen, © 1986 by Henri J.M. Nouwen. Used by permission of Doubleday, a division of Random House, Inc. Also published as In the House of the Lord by Darton, Longman and Todd in the United Kingdom.

Clowning in Rome by Henri J.M. Nouwen, © 1979 by Henri J.M. Nouwen. Used by permission of Doubleday, a division of Random House, Inc. Also published by Darton, Longman and Todd in the United Kingdom.

Compassion by Henri J.M. Nouwen, D. Morrison and D. McNeill © 1982 by Donald P. McNeill, Douglas A. Morrison and Henri J.M. Nouwen. Used by permission of Doubleday, a division of Random House, Inc.

The Return of the Prodigal Son by Henri J.M. Nouwen, © 1992 by Henri J.M. Nouwen. Used by permission of Doubleday, a division of Random House, Inc. Also published by Darton, Longman and Todd in the United Kingdom.

The Inner Voice of Love by Henri J.M. Nouwen, © 1996 by Henri J.M. Nouwen. Used by permission of Doubleday, a division of Random House, Inc. Also published by Darton, Longman and Todd in the United Kingdom.

Reaching Out by Henri J.M. Nouwen, © 1986. Used by permission of Zondervan.

The Path of Waiting by Henri J.M. Nouwen. Used by permission of The Crossroad Publishing Company. Also published as part of *Finding My Way Home* by Darton, Longman and Todd.

Introduction

Henri Nouwen wrote his books to the rhythm of the liturgical year, just as his spiritual inspiration, Vincent van Gogh, painted landscapes that reflected the rotation of the earth's cycle. From the moment van Gogh left Paris to seek new pastures in the south of France, he felt compelled to capture the mood of the seasons. As soon as he arrived in Arles in the early part of 1888, he noticed the effect of the climate on the surrounding countryside. First, he found blossoming almond twigs and brought them indoors for closer study; then he started to marvel at the fields in springtime. Painting meadows of buttercups, yellow wheat fields and orchards decked in their pink and white blooms, van Gogh gradually came to understand the more subtle cadences of nature. Drawn to the strong light of Provence and the warmth of its colours, he followed the same dawn-to-dusk routines as the peasants who became his artistic subjects. This environment offered both stability and inspiration:

> Why move about much? When I see the orchards again, shan't I be in a better condition, and won't it be something

new, a renewed attack on a new season, on the same subject? And the same for the whole year, for harvesttime, and the vineyards, for everything.[1]

Van Gogh's work fell into a number of phases, one of which involved the painting of landscapes on the theme of the seasons. His original idea had been to represent each season by a pair of complementary colours. Now, putting down roots in the south, he would try to bring the project to fruition:

> Will my work really be worse because, by staying in the same place, I shall see the seasons pass and repass over the same subjects, seeing again the same orchards in the spring, the same fields of wheat in summer? . . . it will mean work of a deeper calm at the end of a certain time.[2]

In March that year van Gogh began work on a series of canvases of blossoming orchards in pinks and greens entitled *Spring*. In June he painted *Summer* in blue and orange. Other seasons followed, their moods captured in varying hues and swirls. Spending long hours in the fields and vineyards, he became a meticulous observer of the seasonal currents of nature. He noted, for example, that the olive tree changed colour through the year but was interdependent on the sky, sun and even the insects hovering around it. The life-cycles of the earth, echoing the spiritual patterns of death and resurrection, put van Gogh in touch with the beauty of the eternal. Listening to the language of nature had a certain sacramental significance with its power to comfort, heal and transform. The painter was unveiling the signs of God, the divine artist.

Little wonder, then, that Henri Nouwen discerned theological insights in his fellow Dutchman's work and claimed him as one of his main spiritual influences. Nouwen drew parallels between the struggles of van Gogh's personal life and the manner of his artistic expression. The "sorrowful, yet always rejoicing" dimension of the canvases mirrored Nouwen's own belief in the co-existence of joy and sadness at every stage of the spiritual journey. Both men wanted their work to *touch* people.

In many of his books, Nouwen disclosed his responses to the spiritual seasons, although they were often delicately woven into the fabric of his text. Praying the liturgical year kept him in touch with eternal verities. Not only was his spiritual life in harmony with the metre of the Church's year, his celebrations of the lives of the saints brought him wisdom and encouragement. In this way, Nouwen lived time in eternity and, like van Gogh, reached a new understanding of God and creation. The choreography of the divine dance was creatively rooted in the rhythm of the seasons, the changing patterns giving birth to a spirituality of hope and healing.

I am writing on the feast or, more strictly, the memorial of St. Francis de Sales, patron saint of writers and journalists. By delightful coincidence, it happens to be the anniversary of Henri Nouwen's birth. It also has a personal significance because it was on this day twelve years ago that I started writing a spiritual journal. On my journalistic and spiritual travels around the world, at different times of the liturgical year, the diary has always travelled in tandem with a paperback from the Nouwen collection.

I have always felt an affinity with the spiritual pattern of the year. I was born late in the evening on the day after Pentecost and, while Monday nights are not particularly renowned for their significance, they have always seemed hallowed to me. As a teenager, serving in the Lady Chapel of St. Andrew's Church, Taunton, England, on Thursday evenings and Saturday mornings, I became familiar with all the feasts of the Christian year. It was there in Somerset, under the inspiration of Father John Squire, that I developed a love of the liturgical year. I remember especially our celebrations of Candlemas when the darkened church would become a sea of flickering lights; the Maundy Thursday procession to the altar of response, adorned by bowls of magnificent lilies; the through-the-night vigil and the starkness of the church the following morning for the Good Friday "Mass of the Pre-Sanctified." Our annual visit to the ruins of Glastonbury Abbey took place on the Feast of the Assumption in August—one year the heavens opened but mass around the altar of the crypt chapel was one of

the most atmospheric I have ever experienced. I have never forgotten also how we would assemble for a requiem mass at the local
crematorium every All Souls' Day to remember all those who had
died during the year. These were formative experiences that rooted me in the liturgical tradition of the Christian Church.
Celebrating the seasons year by year with my friends at St.
Andrew's (many of whom are, sadly, no longer with us) gave me
glimpses of the eternal that have never dulled. Although my pilgrimage has since taken me to new horizons, I shall always be
grateful to this loving parish for providing me with a strong spiritual foundation. My journals are strewn with fragments of nostal-
gic dreams about my formation there.

A few years ago, Father John very generously presented me with
all the sermons he had ever preached. As I began to rediscover
homilies that had inspired me in my youth, I was struck by their
remarkable resemblance to the writings of Henri Nouwen—even
though Father John had never read Nouwen during his ministry
and Nouwen had never heard Father John preach. At some mysterious level, it seemed my first parish priest had been sowing the
seeds of a spirituality that would one day flower in and through my
work on Nouwen. Like the Dutch priest, Father John had lived the
liturgical year sensitively and imaginatively, and his sermons on
"the great mysteries of our faith" were often inspired by the festi-
vals we celebrated. In one reflection on the mystery of the
Ascension, he spoke of heaven as "that state where God eternally
is and where God may be eternally possessed."

The word "season" comes in fact from a Latin root meaning "to
sow." Living the Church's year is a process of growth, even a trans-
formational experience. It engages with an entirely different
rhythm, marching to the beat of a different drum. It is a journey
from *chronos*, the chronological world of clocks and calendars, to
kairos, time viewed as opportunity or encounter. As the Benedictine
monk David Steindl-Rast explains: "Eternity is the opposite of
time: It is no time. It is, as Augustine said, 'The now that does not
pass away.' We cannot reach that now by proceeding in mere

chronological sequence, yet it is accessible at any moment as the mysterious fullness of time."[3]

In my life as a journalist, I have always kept my spiritual travelogue close. It is not always possible to lead a conventional liturgical life when you are regularly on the road or in the air but Nouwen's meditations on the liturgy have spoken to me more profoundly than a brief note of explanation in a prayer book or missal. It is so evident that he *lived* the seasons and discerned their eternal significance. His words have enabled me to synchronize my spiritual and journalistic lives. Whether I've been standing silently at Ground Zero on Good Friday, eating decorated eggs with the monks of Mount Athos in Greece during Eastertide, or singing carols beside the Shepherds' Fields of Bethlehem at Christmas, I have been aware of Nouwen's liturgical influence on my own spiritual pilgrimage.

With their different atmospheres and messages, the seasons enabled Nouwen to filter the light and the shade of his own experiences in his restless search for God. When I interviewed him for BBC Radio, I was struck by the way in which he clearly needed to get in touch with what he lived, just as van Gogh had felt it necessary to connect with peasant life in the fields of Provence. "I have always felt that, if you want to talk about your faith, you have to be able to talk about your doubt," Nouwen told me on the Feast of St. Augustine of Hippo: "If you want to talk about hope, you have to talk about despair. If you want to talk about joy, you have to talk about darkness. If you want to speak about salvation, or redemption or freedom, it's very important that you're willing to speak about what you're being redeemed from and what you're being set free from. The spiritual life is a constant choice to let your negative experiences become an opportunity for conversion or renewal."[4] The liturgical year helped Nouwen embrace these polarities and offer hope, just as van Gogh had managed to convey the integration of the seasons and their expectancy through such paintings as "Branches of Almond Tree in Blossom," where new life breaks through from wintry branches against the most radiant blue sky he ever painted.

In one of his early books, Nouwen spoke about our lives vibrat-
ing between two darknesses. "We hesitantly come forth out of the
darkness of birth and slowly vanish into the darkness of death. We
move from dust to dust, from unknown to unknown, from mystery
to mystery."[5] Celebration is only possible "through the deep realization that life and death are never found completely separate."[6]
It can only be realised where fear and love, joy and sorrow, tears
and smiles exist together. Celebrating means "the affirmation of
the present, which becomes fully possible only by remembering the
past and expecting more to come in the future."[7] Many years later,
another book provided a platform for him to proclaim celebrations
taking place at a L'Arche community in France:

> There are always flowers on the table, and often candles or
> napkins with special names. At first I thought of them as
> ways of breaking the dull routine of the weeks and
> months. But I soon realized that here, where people are so
> obviously broken and in need of healing, no day is lived
> without a glimpse of new hope, without the sound of a
> voice that speaks of love, or without the sense that some-
> where among us there is a place that can be fully trusted.
> Whether Brad has his birthday or St. Francis his feast day,
> whether Alain is leaving or Emile is coming back, whether
> Advent is starting or Lent is ending, whether Sylvia has lost
> her mother or Gerard had a new baby sister; yes, whether
> the Lord dies on the Cross or rises from the dead—all must
> be lifted up and celebrated in an unceasing song of joy, the
> joy of a life that no illness or death can destroy.

> Celebration is not just a way to make people feel good for
> a while; it is the way in which faith in the God of life is
> lived out, through both laughter and tears. Thus celebra-
> tion goes beyond ritual, custom, and tradition. It is the
> unceasing affirmation that underneath all the ups and
> downs of life there flows a solid current of joy.[8]

In published correspondence to his teenage nephew around the same period, it is clear that Nouwen believes that liturgical celebrations give a defining character to his Christian pilgrimage:

When I started writing to you, Lent had just begun. I thought then that I'd be able to send you one letter a week. But I seem to have so much to do here in Trosly that I've not been able to live up to my good intentions. It took me five weeks in all to write my letter about the descending way of Jesus. In the meantime, Easter has come round again. It makes me realize how much I am influenced by the liturgical seasons![9]

Later he adds:

To listen to the Church is to listen to the Lord of the Church. Specifically, this means taking part in the Church's liturgical life. Advent, Christmas, Lent, Easter, Ascension, and Pentecost; these seasons and feasts teach you to know Jesus better and better, and unite you more and more intimately with the divine life he offers you in the Church.[10]

But in *Reaching Out* he indicates that his relationship to those who have feast days is somewhat ambivalent:

The really great saints of history don't ask for imitation. Their way was unique and cannot be repeated. But they invite us into their lives and offer a hospitable place for our own search. Some turn us off and make us feel uneasy; others even irritate us, but among the many great spiritual men and women of history we may find a few, or maybe just one or two, who speak the language of our heart and give us courage. These are our guides. Not to be imitated but to help us live our lives just as authentically as they lived theirs.[11]

Furthermore, in his monastic journal, *The Genesee Diary,* Nouwen discloses his unease with certain celebrations in the Church, confessing the difficulty he experiences with feasts honouring the Holy Trinity, the Blessed Sacrament and the Sacred Heart:

> They seem to arise out of a devotional period of the history of the Church in which I have a hard time feeling at home. It always seemed to me that the mystery of the Triune God, of the Divine presence in the Eucharist, and of the love of Christ for people are such realities of the Christian life that you cannot set a special day aside to celebrate them. Certainly a special Sunday for the Eucharist never appealed to me.[12]

Yet, later in the diary, he laments the under-celebration of Thanksgiving Day in the community. Thanksgiving is the day Americans know how to celebrate best, he points out. It is a family day, a day of hospitality, a day of gratitude. But not at the Abbey of the Genesee:

> It is significant that the wine which was given to the monastery for Thanksgiving was used instead for the feast of Christ the King. Except for cranberry sauce—without turkey!—dinner had little to do with Thanksgiving. I keep wondering why monks don't seem to be interested in national feast days. I had expected thanksgiving to be celebrated as a great feast, especially since it is the feast in which deep national and deep religious sentiments emerge. But although Anthony had made a beautiful display of harvest grain and fruit under the altar, although Father Marcellus had us listen to Beethoven's Sixth Symphony during dinner, and although the Mass was the Mass of Thanksgiving, you could sense that the monks were not really celebrating as on Pentecost, on Assumption Day, or All Saints' Day. Maybe they resent the fact that the Pilgrims were not Catholics! Maybe, indeed, Thanksgiving is more a Protestant feast in history and character. Maybe

it is just hard to celebrate Thanksgiving without your family.[13]

There are other examples where he naturally integrates his liturgical sensibilities with his theological awareness. For example, in *Adam*, a tribute to a young man with severe developmental disabilities, Nouwen writes about his friend through the lenses of desert, ministry, passion, death and resurrection which lead him to a more profound understanding of the Gospel message. The presence of Adam enables Nouwen to adjust to a slower rhythm of life, where he connects with sacred time and learns to speak with the language of the heart.

I first became interested in compiling a book like this while researching my portrait of Nouwen, *Wounded Prophet*.[14] In Nouwen's archives (then housed at Yale Divinity School but now at the University of St. Michael's College, Toronto), I came across old sermons on a range of liturgical themes. Some were immaculately handwritten, others typed. I remember unearthing one address, "The Birth of Christ," written back in 1964. It particularly amused me that, after reproducing the nativity narrative from the Gospel of Luke, Nouwen had posed his congregation a question: "Who is the reporter? Who wrote this highly reserved but loaded account?" There were also homilies for "Advent" and "Ash Wednesday," as well as a paper on "Liturgy as Hospitality," in which he argued that liturgical ministry should always be "revealing, uniting and witnessing," a view certainly borne out by his subsequent seasonal reflections.

I have divided this ecumenical book into nine liturgical sections to reflect the emphasis Nouwen gave in his writings to certain celebrations in the calendar. They deviate a little from the traditional pattern. In each chapter, I have chosen meaningful passages from Nouwen's published writings to convey the spirit of the season. There are also reflections for feast days which, depending on the date of Easter, tend to fall within a particular season. I have grouped these largely with months in mind. For example, saints' days for March are included under Lent, while feasts for August,

September and October may be found under "Transfiguration."
Here and there you may think a certain feast should be under a different season. St. Andrew's Day, for example, is often celebrated at
Advent but appears here under "Recollection," which groups all
the significant days in November. All the major feasts are featured,
as well as Nouwen's thoughts on certain saints who captured his
imagination. The choice of headings is mine.

This is the first time that Henri Nouwen's liturgical writings for
an entire year have been published in one volume. While all the
material comes from Nouwen's well-known titles, there is little rep-
etition of sequences which have already appeared in compilations
or texts which focused on only one part of the Christian year. I
hope this book will become a close companion as you contemplate
the Christian year. Its intention is to encourage you to live the liturgical seasons at a more profound level of being. Nouwen's writings
on Lent, for example, cannot be isolated from a personal journey
of repentance and should influence the process of spiritual reintegration during this time of the year. You may care to use the selections alongside the appointed readings for the Church's year or
step back from traditional prayer books and enter into the mystery
of each cycle with Nouwen alone as your guide. Whichever way
you choose, the texts should gradually cultivate within you a deeper appreciation of sacred time and lead (as Nouwen said of van
Gogh's art) not only to "a new way of seeing but also to a new way
of living."[15]

Notes

1. Letter 505, as quoted in Cliff Edwards, *Van Gogh and God* (Loyola University
   Press, 1989), p.109.
2. Letter 535, *ibid.*
3. David Steindl-Rast OSB with Sharon Lebell, *The Music of Silence*,
   (HarperSanFrancisco, 1995), p.12.
4. Interview took place on 28 August 1992, in Northampton and was broadcast
   on BBC Radio 4's *Seeds of Faith* series on 11 July 1993.
5. Henri J.M. Nouwen, *Creative Ministry* (Image, 1991), p. 94.
6. *ibid.*, pp. 94–5.
7. *ibid.*, p.100.

8. Henri J.M. Nouwen, *In the House of the Lord* (Darton, Longman and Todd Ltd, 1986), pp. 66–7.
9. Henri J.M. Nouwen, *Letters to Marc about Jesus* (Darton, Longman and Todd Ltd, 1988), p. 46.
10. *ibid.*, pp. 75–6.
11. Henri J.M. Nouwen, *Reaching Out* (Fount Paperbacks, 1980), p. 128.
12. Henri J.M. Nouwen, *The Genesee Diary* (Image, 1989), pp. 35–6.
13. *ibid.*, p. 187.
14. Michael Ford, *Wounded Prophet, A Portrait of Henri J.M. Nouwen* (Darton, Longman and Todd Ltd, 1999).
15. Henri J.M. Nouwen, foreword to Cliff Edwards, *Van Gogh and God* (Loyola University Press, 1989), p. xi.

Advent

Season of Waiting

Advent

As we embark on our liturgical journey with Henri Nouwen, we know we can take our time. We are in no rush. Advent is essentially a season of patient waiting, even though such a discipline did not come naturally to our spiritual guide. Above all, Nouwen invites us to trust with open hands and to follow the example of Mary who waited lovingly for something to happen, even though what was about to take place might not have seemed natural to her. When we live in sacred time, we are able to take risks without worrying about the consequences. For Nouwen, faithful waiting is the antidote to fear and self-doubt. It is believing God can accomplish in us something greater than our imaginings.

I remember the Advent we spent waiting and watching at my father's bedside. Aged just forty-nine, he had been diagnosed with a brain tumour only weeks before. One month a lecturer with a zest for living, the next a patient with an acceptance of dying. A man who had entered the teaching profession as second career and never looked back, he was devoted to his students. Then, almost overnight, everything changed: an emergency hospital admission, surgery, radiotherapy, and long hours of waiting and wondering.

27

Yet in those swift but terrible weeks, as winter storms howled outside, my father seemed to grow spiritually with an inner awareness that, whatever happened, he was held safe. As his body grew weaker, he trusted with open hands. God would not abandon him. Despite the fear and uncertainty we all felt, there were also glimpses of hope and eternity.

Through the darkness of Advent, we too move towards the light.

Derived from a Latin root, Advent means "coming" or "arrival." Lasting only four weeks, it is traditionally a season of quiet and joyful expectancy. The trees in the northern hemisphere may be barren but we do not lose hope. Advent has a two-fold character: a time of preparation for the festival of the Nativity when the first coming of God's Son to the world is recalled and a period of reflection pointing us to Christ's second coming at the end of time. This is a season for prophecy, calling us to conversion, preparation and a constant sense of watchfulness.

The following extracts from Nouwen's writings include material from his monastic journal, *The Genesee Diary*, written during his time as a temporary Trappist; his diary, *¡Gracias!*, an account of his spell as a missionary priest in Latin America; and a small book, *The Path of Waiting*, published the year before he died. Together they can help us live this season of Advent, not as over-burdened slaves to a consumerist Christmas already in celebration, but as trusting pilgrims waiting in the dark. In strength or in sickness, we wait freely and hopefully for a gift from eternity to be born within us.

WAITING OPEN-ENDEDLY

I have found it very important in my own life to let go of my wishes and start hoping. It was only when I was willing to let go of wishes that something really new, something beyond my own expectations, could happen to me. Just imagine what Mary was actually saying in the words, "I am the handmaid of the Lord. Let what you have said be done to me" (Luke 1:38). She was saying, "I don't know what this all means, but I trust that good things will happen." She trusted so deeply that her waiting was open to all possibilities. And she did not want to control them. She believed that when she listened carefully, she could trust what was going to happen.

To wait open-endedly is an enormously radical attitude toward life. It is trusting that something will happen to us that is far beyond our own imaginings. It is giving up control over our future and letting God define our life. It is living with the conviction that God moulds us according to God's love and not according to our fear. The spiritual life is a life in which we wait, actively present to the moment, expecting that new things will happen to us, new things that are far beyond our own imagination or prediction. That, indeed, is a very radical stance in a world preoccupied with control

—The Path of Waiting

WAITING TOGETHER

Waiting is first of all a waiting together. One of the most beautiful passages of Scripture is Luke 1:39–56, which tells us about Mary's visit to Elizabeth. What happened when Mary received the words of promise? She went to Elizabeth. Something was happening to Elizabeth as well as to Mary. But how could they live that out?

I find the meeting of these two women very moving, because Elizabeth and Mary came together and enabled each other to wait. Mary's visit made Elizabeth aware of what she was waiting for. The child leapt for joy in her. Mary affirmed Elizabeth's waiting. And then Elizabeth said to Mary, "Blessed is she who believed that the promise made her by the Lord would be fulfilled" (Luke 1:45). And Mary responded, "My soul proclaims the greatness of the Lord" (Luke 1:46). She burst into joy herself. These two women created space for each other to wait: They affirmed for each other that something was happening worth waiting for.

Here we see a model for the Christian community. It is a community of support, celebration, and affirmation in which we can lift up what has already begun in us. The visit of Elizabeth to Mary is one of the Bible's most beautiful expressions of what it means to form community, to be together, gathered around a promise, affirming what is happening among us.

—The Path of Waiting

WAITING IN FEAR

For many people, waiting is a dry desert between where they are and where they want to go. And people do not like such a place. They want to get out of it by doing something.

In our particular historical situation, waiting is even more difficult because we are so fearful. One of the most pervasive emotions in the atmosphere around us is fear. People are afraid—afraid of inner feelings, afraid of other people, and also afraid of the future. Fearful people have a hard time waiting, because when we are afraid we want to get away from where we are. But if we cannot flee, we may fight instead. Many of our destructive acts come from the fear that something harmful will be done to us. And if we take a broader perspective—that not only individuals but whole communities and nations might be afraid of being harmed—we can understand how hard it is to wait and how tempting it is to act. Here are the roots of a "first strike" approach to others. People who live in a world of fear are more likely to make aggressive, hostile, destructive responses than people who are not so frightened. The more afraid we are, the harder waiting becomes. That is why waiting is such an unpopular attitude for many people.

It impresses me, therefore, that all the figures who appear on the first pages of Luke's Gospel are waiting. Zechariah and Elizabeth are waiting. Mary is waiting. Simeon and Anna, who were there at the temple when Jesus was brought in, are waiting. The whole opening scene of the good news is filled with waiting people. And right at the beginning all those people in some way or another hear the words, "Do not be afraid. I have something good to say to you." These indicate that Zechariah, Elizabeth, Mary, Simeon, and Anna are waiting for something new and good to happen to them.

—The Path of Waiting

SEEDS OF WAITING

Waiting, as we see it in the people on the first pages of the Gospel, is waiting with a sense of promise. "Zechariah, your wife Elizabeth is to bear you a son." "Mary, listen! You are to conceive and bear a son" (Luke 1:13, 31, JB). People who wait have received a promise that allows them to wait. They have received something that is at work in them, like a seed that has started to grow. This is very important. We can really wait only if what we are waiting for has already begun for us. So waiting is never a movement from nothing to something. It is always a movement from something to something more.

—*The Path of Waiting*

NURTURING THE MOMENT

A waiting person is a patient person. The word "patience" means the willingness to stay where we are and live the situation out to the full in the belief that something hidden there will manifest itself to us. Impatient people are always expecting the real thing to happen somewhere else and therefore want to go elsewhere. The moment is empty. But patient people dare to stay where they are. Patient living means to live actively in the present and wait there. Waiting, then, is not passive. It involves nurturing the moment, as a mother nurtures the child that is growing in her womb.

—*The Path of Waiting*

A HIDDEN PROMISE

"A shoot shall sprout from the stump of Jesse, and from his roots a bud shall blossom. The spirit of the Lord shall rest upon him . . ." (Isa. 11:12).

. . . Our salvation comes from something small, tender, and vulnerable, something hardly noticeable. God, who is the Creator of the Universe, comes to us in smallness, weakness, and hiddenness.

I find this a hopeful message. Somehow, I keep expecting loud and impressive events to convince me and others of God's saving power; but over and over again, I am reminded that spectacles, power plays, and big events are the ways of the world. Our temptation is to be distracted by them, and made blind to the "shoot that shall sprout from the stump."

When I have no eyes for the small signs of God's presence—the smile of a baby, the carefree play of children, the words of encouragement and gestures of love offered by friends—I will always remain tempted to despair.

The small child of Bethlehem, the unknown young man of Nazareth, the rejected preacher, the naked man on the cross, *he* asks for my full attention. The work of our salvation takes place in the midst of a world that continues to shout, scream, and overwhelm us with its claims and promises. But the promise is hidden in the shoot that sprouts from the stump, a shoot that hardly anyone notices.

—*¡Gracias!*

A GREAT EXPECTATION

In Isaiah I read: "Young men may grow tired and weary, youths may stumble, but those who hope in Yahweh renew their strength, they put out wings like eagles. They run and do not grow weary, walk and never tire" (40:30–1). The words of God are indeed like eagles' wings. Maybe I can deepen my hope in God by giving more time and attention to his words . . . .

The words about God's coming not only remind us that God will appear, but also that he will slowly transform our whole being into expectation. Then we will no longer have expectations but be expectation, then all we are has become "waiting."

—*The Genesee Diary*

CONTEMPLATING CHRIST'S COMING

The expectation of Advent is anchored in the event of God's incarnation. The more I come in touch with what happened in the past, the more I come in touch with what is to come. The Gospel not only reminds me of what took place but also of what will take place. In the contemplation of Christ's first coming, I can discover the signs of his second coming. By looking back in meditation, I can look forward in expectation. By reflection, I can project; by conserving the memory of Christ's birth, I can progress to the fulfilment of his kingdom. I am struck by the fact that the prophets speaking about the future of Israel always kept reminding their people of God's great works in the past. They could look forward with confidence because they could look backward with awe to Yahweh's great deeds. . . .

I pray that Advent will offer me the opportunity to deepen my memory of God's great deeds in time and will set me free to look forward with courage to the fulfilment of time by him who came and is still to come.

—*The Genesee Diary*

PREPARING FOR JUDGEMENT

John Eudes said . . . that we should desire not only the first coming of Christ in his lowly human gentleness but also his second coming as the judge of our lives. I sensed that the desire for Christ's judgement is a real aspect of holiness and realized how little that desire was mine.

In his Advent sermon, Guerric of Igny understands that it is not easy to desire with fervour this second coming. Therefore, he says, if we cannot prepare ourselves for the day of judgement by desire, let us at least prepare ourselves by fear. Now I see better how part of Christian maturation is the slow but persistent deepening of fear to the point where it becomes desire. The fear of God is not in contrast with his mercy. Therefore, words such as fear and desire, justice and mercy have to be relearned and reunderstood when we use them in our intimate relationship with the Lord.

—*The Genesee Diary*

JOYFUL ANTICIPATION

We are joyful already now because we know that the Lord will come. Our expectation leads to joy and our joy to a desire to give to others. Real joy always wants to share. It belongs to the nature of joy to communicate itself to others and to invite others to take part in the gifts we have received.

Advent is indeed a time of joyful waiting and joyful giving. John Eudes observed how much this mood is also part of our whole society. The period before Christmas has that remarkable quality of joy that seems to touch not only Christians but all who live in our society. When you, as a Westerner, live in another society, such as the Japanese society, where Advent and Christmas do not exist as universal events, you realize the lack of this joyful anticipation most painfully.

—*The Genesee Diary*

ETERNAL LIGHT

During the last week of Advent it seems as if the liturgy can no longer hide the excitement about the coming of the Lord and bursts forth in anticipatory joy. During Vespers the "O" antiphons express unrestrained exhilaration. "O Wisdom that proceeds from the mouth of the Most High, O Adonai and leader of the House of Israel, O Root of Jesse who stands as the ensign of the peoples, O Key of David and Sceptre of the House of Israel, O Orient, Splendour of eternal Light, O King of nations, the One for whom they long, O Emmanuel, the Expectation and Saviour of the nations—come to us, O Lord, Our God." Every evening between December 17 and 24 a new "O" is sung and, slowly, waiting and welcoming, expecting and seeing, hoping and receiving, future and present merge into one song of praise to the Lord who has visited his people.

What strikes me is that waiting is a period of learning. The longer we wait the more we hear about him for whom we are waiting. As the Advent weeks progress, we hear more and more about the beauty and splendour of the One who is to come. The Gospel passages read during Mass all talk about the events before Jesus' birth and the people ready to receive him. In the other readings Isaiah heaps prophecy on prophecy to strengthen and deepen our hope, and the songs, lessons, commentaries, and antiphons all compete in their attempt to set the stage for the Lord who is to come.

There is a stark beauty about it all. But is this not a preparation that can only lead to anticlimax? I don't think so. Advent does not lead to nervous tension stemming from expectation of something spectacular about to happen. On the contrary, it leads to a growing inner stillness and joy allowing me to realize that he for whom I am waiting has already arrived and speaks to me in the silence of my heart. Just as a mother feels the child grow in her and is not surprised on the day of the birth but joyfully receives the one she learned to know during her waiting, so Jesus can be born in my life slowly and steadily and be received as the one I learned to know while waiting.

—*The Genesee Diary*

COME, LORD JESUS

O Lord, how hard it is to accept your way. You come to me as a small, powerless child born away from home. You live for me as a stranger in your own land. You die for me as a criminal outside the walls of a city, rejected by your own people, misunderstood by your friends, and feeling abandoned by your God.

As I prepare to celebrate your birth, I am trying to feel loved, accepted, and at home in this world, and I am trying to overcome the feelings of alienation and separation which continue to assail me. But I wonder now if my deep sense of homelessness does not bring me closer to you than my occasional feelings of belonging. Where do I truly celebrate your birth: in a cozy home or in an unfamiliar house, among welcoming friends or among unknown strangers, with feelings of well-being or with feelings of loneliness?

I do not have to run away from those experiences that are closest to yours. Just as you do not belong to this world, so I do not belong to this world. Every time I feel this way I have an occasion to be grateful and to embrace you better and taste more fully your joy and peace.

Come, Lord Jesus, and be with me where I feel poorest. I trust that this is the place where you will find your manger and bring your light. Come, Lord Jesus, come. Amen.

—*The Road to Daybreak*

Advent Feasts

NICHOLAS, Bishop of Myra, c. 326 CE
(6 December)

I vividly remember the St. Nicholas's celebrations in Holland. They were evenings of gifts, surprises, rhymes, and jokes, and, of course, the visit of the Holy Man himself, accompanied by the "black Peter"! No gifts at Christmas, but countless gifts on St. Nicholas's Eve! I have many childhood memories connected with this beautiful event. All are gentle, good, and rich with affection.

—*Sabbatical Journey*

Today in Holland everyone is exchanging presents. St. Nicholas evening—the most playful, folkloric celebration of Holland. Full of surprises. The children are in the centre, but nobody is excluded from attention. I miss it tonight. Many Dutchmen who are not in Holland will miss it also or will create their own St. Nicholas evening with other Dutchmen whom they gather together.

—*The Genesee Diary*

IMMACULATE CONCEPTION OF THE
BLESSED VIRGIN MARY
(8 December)

In this feast it seems that all the quiet beauty of Advent suddenly bursts forth into exuberance and exultation. In Mary we see all the beauty of Advent concentrated. She is the one in whom the waiting of Israel is most fully and most purely manifested; she is the last of the remnant of Israel for whom God shows his mercy and fulfills his promises; she is the faithful one who believed that the promise made to her by the Lord would be fulfilled; she is the lowly handmaid, the obedient servant, the quiet contemplative. She indeed is the most prepared to receive the Lord.

It seems that there is no better time to celebrate this feast than during these Advent days. It is the celebration of the beauty of she who is ready to receive the Lord. It is like admiring the palace where the King will enter, the room to which the bridegroom will come, the garden where the great encounter will take place.

I think of the painting on the ceiling of the Sistine Chapel where God stretches out his hand to Adam to call him to life. How beautifully humanity is created. Now God again is stretching out his arm to she who waits for his touch by which humanity is re-created even more beautifully. The celebration of this feast is the anticipation of the great event of Christmas. It makes me feel like a child on the evening before a wedding, full of joy and anticipation. I have already seen the bridal gown. I have already smelled the flowers. I have already heard the wedding song. There is no longer any doubt. Tomorrow it will surely happen; everything is ready to be fulfilled.

This feast day gives Advent its true character. It is indeed primarily a season of joy. It is not, like Lent, primarily a time of penance. No, there is too much anticipation for that. All-overriding is the experience of joy.

—*The Genesee Diary*

JOHN OF THE CROSS, Poet, Teacher of the Faith, 1591
(14 December)

Today is the feast of St. John of the Cross, the sixteenth-century Spanish mystic who speaks to me with great power. Not only did

St. John experience oppression, humiliation, and imprisonment in his attempts to reform the Carmelite Order, but in the midst of his agony he experienced God's love as a purifying flame and was able to express this love in the most profound mystical poetry.

St. John reveals the intimate connection between resistance and contemplation. He reminds us that true resistance against the powers of destruction can be a lifelong commitment only when it is fed by an ardent love for the God of justice and peace. The ultimate goal of true resistance is not simply to do away with poverty, injustice, and oppression, but to make visible the all-restoring love of God. The true mystic always searches for this Divine knowledge in the midst of darkness. St. John sings "the Song of the Soul Delighted by the Knowledge of God" (*el cantar del alma que se huelga de conocer a Dios*). He sings this song "though it is night" (*aunque es noche*).

In the midst of our darkness . . . St. John of the Cross sings of a light too bright for our eyes to see. In this divine Light we find the source of our whole being. In this Light we live, even when we cannot grasp it. The Light sets us free to resist all evil and to be faithful in the darkness, always waiting for the day in which God's presence will be revealed to us in all its glory.

—*¡Gracias!*

Christmas

Season of Peace

Christmas

Divine fragility is a theme permeating Henri Nouwen's reflections on Christmas. He sees direct connections between the vulnerable Christchild and the presence of God among the suffering, the hungry and the marginalized. During this season of peace, we welcome God into our hearts, not as a distant king or a moral watchdog, but as an intimate companion from heaven, ready to join us on our journey. As an old prayer puts it: "Fill our hearts with the quiet silence of that night on which your almighty Word leapt down out of your royal throne, and came to visit us in great humility."

Christmas spans twelve days, a time when we acclaim the mystery of the incarnation: God-with-us. It is a season that opens us up to the presence of God in new and unexpected guises. Reporting from the warmer climes of Bethlehem at this time of year, I was especially moved by the story of a young Greek Orthodox Christian I met in the nearby West Bank city of Beit Sahour. Greeting me from a wheelchair, he explained that, when he was eighteen, he had been shot at by the Israeli special forces and been hit several times. One bullet had penetrated his spine and, as a result, he had suffered paraplegia from the chest down. But through his disability he had become an international ambassador for peace on behalf of the YMCA.

Even though he still had great difficulty forgiving the soldiers who had fired at him, he said the shooting had not clouded his inner vision to bring hope to the world. "We say here that the hit which doesn't kill makes us stronger," he told me in the bright afternoon sunshine. "The hit I got might not have killed me but it turned my life upside down. It made me stronger in continuing to fight for justice and freedom."

In the short time I was in the company of this smiling Palestinian, I sensed that a body violated by gunfire had been mysteriously touched by divine life.

Christmas brings peace when we inspire others through our vulnerability.

Henri Nouwen writes about the spiritual significance of such fragility. The Prince of Peace does not take refuge in lavishly decorated hotels or seek hospitality at sumptuous dinner tables. He chooses the way of poverty and humiliation. Nouwen's writings on Christmas were composed not only during his time with monks and missionaries but when he was feeling displaced himself. Moving from the familiarity of academic life to the unknown territory of L'Arche, he knew feelings of alienation and insecurity. But he discovered that living on the edge brought him much closer to the heart of the vulnerable child.

THE CHRIST-CHILD WITHIN

I think that we have hardly thought through the immense implications of the mystery of the incarnation. Where is God? God is where we are weak, vulnerable, small, and dependent. God is where the poor are, the hungry, the handicapped, the mentally ill, the elderly, the powerless. How can we come to know God when our focus is elsewhere, on success, influence, and power? I increasingly believe that our faithfulness will depend on our willingness to go where there is brokenness, loneliness, and human need. If the church has a future it is a future with the poor in whatever form. Each one of us is very seriously searching to live and grow in this belief, and by friendship we can support each other. I realize that the only way for us to stay well in the midst of the many "worlds" is to stay close to the small, vulnerable child that lives in our hearts and in every other human being. Often we do not know that the Christ child is within us. When we discover him we can truly rejoice.

—*Sabbatical Journey*

THE COMPANION OF CHRISTMAS

God came to us because he wanted to join us on the road, to listen to our story, and to help us realize that we are not walking in circles but moving towards the house of peace and joy. This is the great mystery of Christmas that continues to give us comfort and consolation: we are not alone on our journey. The God of love who gave us life sent us his only Son to be with us at all times and in all places, so that we never have to feel lost in our struggles but always can trust that he walks with us.

The challenge is to let God be who he wants to be. A part of us clings to our aloneness and does not allow God to touch us where we are most in pain. Often we hide from him precisely those places in ourselves where we feel guilty, ashamed, confused, and lost. Thus we do not give him a chance to be with us where we feel most alone.

Christmas is the renewed invitation not to be afraid and to let him—whose love is greater than our own hearts and minds can comprehend—be our companion.

—*¡Gracias!*

IN PLACE OF JOY

For many, Christmas is no longer the day to celebrate the mystery of the birth of God among us, the God hidden in the wounds of humanity. It is no longer the day of the child, awaited with prayer and repentance, contemplated with watchful attentiveness, and remembered in liturgical solemnity, joyful song, and peaceful family meals. Instead, Christmas has become a time when companies send elaborate gifts to their clients to thank them for their business, when post offices work overtime to process an overload of greeting cards, when immense amounts of money are spent on food and drink, and socializing becomes a full-time activity. There are trees, decorated streets, sweet tunes in the supermarkets, and children saying to their parents: "I want this and I want that." The shallow happiness of busy people often fills the place meant to experience the deep, lasting joy of Emmanuel, God-with-us.

—In the House of the Lord

MAJESTY AND POVERTY

Shortly before 10:00 a.m. my father and I took a cab to the cathedral (Das Munster). It was packed, but I was able to get my father a seat in the front row, which was reserved for the elderly. The service was festive, solemn, and very "royal"—processions, incense, candles, and many servers.

The archbishop of Freiburg presided and gave the homily. "Does this cathedral help or hinder us in understanding the mystery of Christmas?" he asked. I was fascinated by the question, since I had just been thinking about the fact that such a hidden and poor event as the birth of Jesus had inspired the creation of such a majestic building and such a rich liturgy. What had all the Gothic splendour, the paintings and sculptures, the robes, staff, mitre, and long ceremonies to do with the little baby born in Bethlehem twenty centuries ago?

—Sabbatical Journey

THE BLESSING OF THE DOLLS

Peter, the Polish priest, and I presided together over the midnight Mass in Temporal. Temporal is a section of Cochabamba that does not have its own church. . . . While celebrating the Eucharist, Peter and I were surrounded by baby dolls, small and large, naked and elaborately dressed, lying on simple cushions or hidden in large glass cases. I never saw so many Jesus-babies together in my life. I soon found out that it belongs to the folk tradition that the baby Jesus has to hear Mass on Christmas day. Therefore families take their Christmas child out of his stable and bring him to church. After Mass, Peter and I were busy for quite a while blessing all the dolls and giving ample attention to the different ways the baby Jesus looked.

But whatever the surprises were, all the people were happy, joyful, and pleased with this holy night. . . . When I looked up to the sky, I saw a splendid firmament richly decorated with the bright stars singing their praises to the newborn child. And we, little people with our candles, rosaries, and dolls, smiled at the heavens and heard the song again: "Glory to God in the highest heaven, and peace to men and women and children who enjoy his favour."

—*¡Gracias!*

A "YES" BEYOND EMOTIONS

Everything was there to make it a splendid Christmas. But I wasn't really there. I felt like a sympathetic observer. I couldn't force myself to feel differently. It just seemed that I wasn't part of it. At times I even caught myself looking at it all like an unbeliever who wonders what everybody is so busy and excited about. Spiritually, this is a dangerous attitude. It creates a certain sarcasm, cynicism, and depression. But I didn't want or choose it. I just found myself in a mental state that I could not move out of by my own force.

Still, in the midst of it all I saw—even though I did not feel—that this day may prove to be a grace after all. Somehow I realized that songs, music, good feelings, beautiful liturgies, nice presents, big dinners, and many sweet words do not make Christmas. Christmas is saying "yes" to something beyond all emotions and feelings. Christmas is saying "yes" to a hope based on God's initiative, which has nothing to do with what I think or feel. Christmas is believing that the salvation of the world is God's work and not mine. Things will never look just right or feel just right. If they did, someone would be lying. The world is not whole, and today I experienced this fact in my own unhappiness. But it is into this broken world that a child is born who is called Son of the Most High, Prince of Peace, Saviour.

I look at him and pray, 'Thank you, Lord, that you came, in-
dependent of my feelings and thoughts. Your heart is greater than
mine.' Maybe a "dry" Christmas, a Christmas without much to
feel or think, will bring me closer to the true mystery of God-
with-us. What it asks is pure, naked faith.

—*The Road to Daybreak*

THE CHANGING LIGHT

How shall I describe this Holy Night? How shall I give expression
to the multitude of feelings and ideas that come together in this
most joyful celebration? This night is the fulfillment of four weeks
of expectation; it is the remembrance of the most intimate mystery
of life, the birth of God in an agonizing world; it is the planting of
the seeds of compassion, freedom and peace in a harsh, unfree,
and hateful society; it is hope in a new earth to come. . . .

The monks smile and embrace me, the night is soft and quiet,
the gentle sounds of the bells during the midnight "Gloria" still
echo in my soul. All is still and quiet now. The branches of the
trees outside are decorated with fresh white snow and the winds
have withdrawn to let us enjoy for a moment the unbelievable
beauty of the night of peace, the Holy Night.

What can I say on a night like this? It is all very small and very
large, very close and very distant, very tangible and very elusive. I
keep thinking about the Christmas scene that Anthony arranged
under the altar. This probably is the most meaningful "crib" I have
ever seen. Three small wood-carved figures made in India: a poor
woman, a poor man, and a small child between them. The carv-
ing is simple, nearly primitive. No eyes, no ears, no mouths, just the
contours of the faces. The figures are smaller than a human hand
—nearly too small to attract attention at all. But then—a beam of
light shines on the three figures and projects large shadows on the
wall of the sanctuary. That says it all. The light thrown on the
smallness of Mary, Joseph, and the Child projects them as large,
hopeful shadows against the walls of our life and our world. While

looking at the intimate scene we already see the first outlines of the majesty and glory they represent. While witnessing the most human of human events, I see the majesty of God appearing on the horizon of my existence. While being moved by the gentleness of these three people, I am already awed by the immense greatness of God's love appearing in my world. Without the radiant beam of light shining into the darkness there is little to be seen. I might just pass by these three simple people and continue to walk in darkness. But everything changes with the light.

—*The Genesee Diary*

LIVING IN SOLIDARITY

As soon as we call God, "God-with-us," we enter into a new relationship of intimacy with him. By calling him Immanuel, we recognize that he has committed himself to live in solidarity with us, to share our joys and pains, to defend and protect us, and to suffer all of life with us. The God-with-us is a close God, a God whom we call our refuge, our stronghold, our wisdom, and even, more intimately, our helper, our shepherd, our love. We will never really know God as a compassionate God if we do not understand with our heart and mind that "he lived among us" (John 1:14).

—*Compassion*

Christmas Feasts

STEPHEN, Deacon, First Martyr
(26 December)

To forgive another person from the heart is an act of liberation. We set that person free from the negative bonds that exist between us. We say, "I no longer hold your offence against you." But there is more. We also free ourselves from the burden of being the "offended one." As long as we do not forgive those who have wounded us, we carry them with us, or worse, pull them as a heavy load. The great temptation is to cling in anger to our enemies and then define ourselves as being offended and wounded by them. Forgiveness therefore liberates not only the other but also ourselves. It is the way to the freedom of the children of God.

—*Bread for the Journey*

JOHN, Apostle and Evangelist
(27 December)

Knowing God's heart means consistently, radically, and very concretely to announce and reveal that God is love and only love, and that every time fear, isolation, or despair begin to invade the human soul this is not something that comes from God . . . very few people know that they are loved without any conditions or limits. This unconditional and unlimited love is what the evangelist John calls God's first love. "Let us love," he says, "because God loved us first" (1 John 4:19). The love that often leaves us doubtful,

51

frustrated, angry, and resentful is the second love, that is to say, the affirmation, affection, sympathy, encouragement, and support that we receive from our parents, teachers, spouses, and friends. We all know how limited, broken, and very fragile that love is. Behind the many expressions of this second love there is always the chance of rejection, withdrawal, punishment, blackmail, violence, and even hatred. Many contemporary movies and plays portray the ambiguities and ambivalences of human relationships, and there are no friendships, marriages, or communities in which the strains and stresses of the second love are not keenly felt. Often it seems that beneath the pleasantries of daily life there are many gaping wounds that carry such names as: abandonment, betrayal, rejection, rupture and loss. These are all the shadow side of the second love and reveal the darkness that never completely leaves the human heart.

The radical good news is that the second love is only a broken reflection of the first love and that the first love is offered to us by a God in whom there are no shadows. Jesus' heart is the incarnation of the shadow-free first love of God. From his heart flow streams of living water. He cries out in a loud voice, "Let anyone who is thirsty come to me! Let anyone who believes in me come and drink" (John 7:37).

—In the Name of Jesus

When St. John says that fear is driven out by perfect love, he points to a love that comes from God, a divine love. He does not speak about human affection, psychological compatibility, mutual attraction, or deep interpersonal feelings. All of that has its virtue and beauty, but the perfect love about which St. John speaks embraces and transcends all feelings, emotions, and passions. The perfect love that drives out all fear is the divine love in which we are invited to participate. The home, the intimate place, the place of true belonging, is therefore not a place made by human hands. It is fashioned for us by God, who came to pitch his tent among us, invite us to his place, and prepare a room for us in his own house.

Words for "home" are often used in the Old and New Testaments. The Psalms are filled with a yearning to dwell in the house of God, to take refuge under God's wings, and to find protection in God's holy temple; they praise God's holy place, God's wonderful tent, God's firm refuge. We might even say that "to dwell in God's house" summarizes all the aspirations expressed in these inspired prayers. It is therefore highly significant that St. John describes Jesus as the Word of God pitching his tent among us (John 1:14).

—In the House of the Lord

THE HOLY INNOCENTS
(28 December)

As we see so many people die at a young age, through wars, starvation, AIDS, street violence and physical and emotional neglect, we often wonder what the value of their short lives is. It seems that their journeys have been cut off before they could reach any of their goals, realise any of their dreams or accomplish any of their tasks. But, short as their lives may have been, they belong to that immense communion of saints, from all times and all places, who stand around the throne of the Lamb dressed in white robes proclaiming the victory of the crucified Christ (see Revelation 7:9).

The story of the innocent children, murdered by King Herod in his attempt to destroy Jesus (see Matthew 2:13–18), reminds us that saintliness is not just for those who lived long and hard-working lives. These children, and many others who died young, are as much witnesses to Jesus as those who accomplished heroic deeds.

—Bread for the Journey

The children always challenge me to live in the present. They want me to be with them here and now, and they find it hard to understand that I might have other things to do or to think about. After all my experiences of psychotherapy, I suddenly have discovered the great healing power of children. Every time Pablito, Johnny, and Maria run up to welcome me, pick up my suitcase, and bring me to my "roof-room," I marvel at their ability to be fully present to me. Their uninhibited expression of affection and their willingness to receive it pull me directly into the moment and invite me to celebrate life where it is found.

. . . I did not know what to expect when I came to Pamplona Alta. I wondered how the poverty, the lack of good food and good housing would affect me; I was afraid of becoming depressed by the misery I would see. But God showed me something else first: affectionate, open, and playful children who are telling me about love and life in ways no book was ever able to do. I now realize that only when I can enter with the children into their joy will I be able to enter also with them into their poverty and pain. God obviously wants me to walk into the world of suffering with a little child on each hand.

—*¡Gracias!*

"Let the little children come to me; do not stop them; for it is to such as these that the kingdom of God belongs. In truth I tell you, anyone who does not welcome the kingdom of God like a little child will never enter it" (Mark 10:14–15).

What is so special about a little child? The little child has nothing to prove, nothing to show, nothing to be proud of. All the child needs to do is to receive the love that is offered. Jesus wants us to receive the love he offers. He wants nothing more than that we allow him to love us and enjoy that love. This is so hard since we always feel that we have to deserve the love offered to us. But Jesus wants to offer that love to us not because we have earned it, but because he has decided to love us independently of any effort on our side. Our own love for each other should flow from that "first love" that is given to us undeserved.

As I was reflecting on Jesus' words, I started to see more clearly how Daybreak could help me not only to receive the little children, but also to become like one of them. The handicapped may be able to show me the way to a second childhood. Indeed, they can reveal to me God's first love. Handicapped people have little, if anything, to show the world. They have no degrees, no reputation, no influence, no connections with influential people; they do not create much, produce much, or earn much. They have to trust that they can receive and give pure love. I have already received so many hugs and kisses here from people who have never heard of me and are not the least impressed by me that I have to start believing that the love they offer is freely given, to be freely received.

—*The Road to Daybreak*

THE NAMING AND CIRCUMCISION OF JESUS
(1 January)

Ministry is acting in the Name of Jesus. When all our actions are in the Name, they will bear fruit for eternal life. To act in the Name of Jesus, however, doesn't mean to act as a representative of Jesus or his spokesperson. It means to act in an intimate communion with him. The Name is like a house, a tent, a dwelling. To act in the Name of Jesus therefore means to act from the place where we are united with Jesus in love.

—*Bread for the Journey*

SOLEMNITY OF MARY, MOTHER OF GOD
(1 January)

The icon of the Virgin of Vladimir has gradually become for me a strong yet gentle invitation to leave the compulsive and divisive milieu of the world, and to enter the liberating and uniting milieu of God. . . . Her eyes look inward and outward at once. They look inward to the heart of God and outward to the heart of the world, thus revealing the unfathomable unity between the Creator and the creation. They see the eternal in the temporal, the lasting in the passing, the divine in the human. Her eyes gaze upon the infinite spaces of the heart where joy and sorrow are no longer contrasting emotions, but are transcended in spiritual unity.

The meaning of Mary's gaze is further accentuated by the bright stars on her forehead and shoulders (only two are visible; one is covered by the child). They not only indicate her virginity before, during, and after the birth of Jesus, but also speak of a divine presence that permeates part of her being. She is completely open to the divine Spirit, making her innermost being completely attentive to the creative power of God. Thus being mother and being virgin are no longer mutually exclusive. On the contrary, they bring each other to completion. Mary's motherhood completes her virginity, and her virginity completes her motherhood. That is why she carries in Greek the highest title that a human being has ever received: Theotokos, "The Bearer of God."

Praying to the Virgin of Vladimir, we learn that although she is not looking at us, she is truly seeing us. She sees us with the same eyes as she sees Jesus. They are the eyes which saw her Lord before she conceived him, contemplated the Word before it became flesh in her and sensed God within before she heard the angel's message. With these eyes the Virgin sees the child. Her gaze is not that of a proud mother of an exceptional baby; she sees him with the faithful eyes of the Mother of God. Before seeing him with the eyes of her body, she saw him with the eyes of faith. That is why the Sacred Liturgy continues to praise Mary as the one who conceived God in her heart before she conceived God in her body.

As Mary sees Jesus, so she sees those who pray to her: not as interesting human beings worthy of her attention, but as people called away from the darkness of sin into the light of faith, called to become daughters and sons of God. It is hard for us to relinquish our worldly identity as noteworthy people and accept our spiritual identity as children of God. We so much want to be looked at that we are ill prepared to be truly seen. But the eyes of the Virgin invite us to let go of our old ways of belonging and accept the good news that we truly belong to God.

—*Behold the Beauty of the Lord*

NEW YEAR'S DAY

A new beginning! We must learn to live each day, each hour, yes, each minute as a new beginning, as a unique opportunity to make everything new. Imagine that we could live each moment as a moment pregnant with new life. Imagine that we could live each day as a day full of promises. Imagine that we could walk through the new year always listening to a voice saying to us: "I have a gift for you and can't wait for you to see it!" Imagine.

Is it possible that our imagination can lead us to the truth of our lives? Yes, it can! The problem is that we allow our past, which becomes longer and longer each year, to say to us: 'You know it all; you have seen it all, be realistic; the future will be just another repeat of the past. Try to survive it as best you can.' There are many cunning foxes jumping on our shoulders and whispering in our ears the great lie: "There is nothing new under the sun . . . don't let yourself be fooled."

When we listen to these foxes, they eventually prove themselves right: our new year, our new day, our new hour become flat, boring, dull, and without anything new.

So what are we to do? First, we must send the foxes back to where they belong: in their foxholes. And then we must open our minds and our hearts to the voice that resounds through the valleys and hills of our life saying: "Let me show you where I live among my people. My name is 'God-with-you.' I will wipe away all the tears from your eyes; there will be no more death, and no more mourning or sadness. The world of the past has gone" (see Revelation 21:2–5).

We must choose to listen to that voice, and every choice will open us a little more to discover the new life hidden in the moment, waiting eagerly to be born.

—Here and Now

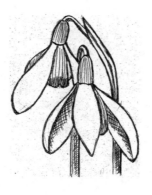

Epiphany

Season of Revelation

Epiphany

The word "epiphany" comes from the Greek *epiphaneia* or *theophaneia*, meaning "appearance" or "manifestation." After the festivities of Christmas, it is the time of the Christian year when we wonder at the revelation of God to the world in Jesus Christ. The Feast of the Epiphany on January 6 symbolises the fact that "the man born to be king" will rule not by force but by love, reigning not from a throne but from a cross. Gold for a king, frankincense for a priest, and myrrh for the one who was to die: the gifts of the wise men foretell that he will be the true king, perfect high priest and supreme savior. The unfolding season honours the public life and witness of Christ, including his baptism in the Jordan, the miracles he performs and his unfailing compassion for others.

Henri Nouwen writes abundantly on these aspects of the spiritual life, seeing Jesus primarily as the revelation of God's unconditional love for all people. Nouwen was always searching for love and belonging in his personal life but, slowly and painfully, came to realize that no one person could ever be expected to emulate the unconditional love of God. Through his gifts of preaching, teaching, writing, and pastoral care, Nouwen unveiled the infinite love of God for others.

But God's compassion is revealed not only by ministers. It is made manifest in and through those who are being visited or ministered too. I think especially of a friend from my home parish. Once a great walker in all winds and weathers, she is now cared for in a local nursing home. Although blind and unable to move far, she continues to radiate the presence of God every time I see her. We hold hands and pray together, yet it is she who is ministering to me, blessing me with the wisdom of age and fidelity. Our meetings take place in sacred time and are sacramental in their intensity. The sky is often brooding as I walk in but invariably more cheerful by the time I leave. After engaging with this person of remarkable faith and devotion, I return to the world of linear time with greater hope and gentleness.

Epiphany is the season of compassionate encounter.

The following selections (including sequences from two of Nouwen's final books, Bread for the Journey and Sabbatical Journey) reveal an eager man almost craving to share his love of Christ with others. While Nouwen was indisputably a charismatic communicator of the Word, he also ministered privately to others at a level of intimacy where wounds could be shared and healed. Many testified to his extraordinary presence. To be in the company of Nouwen was a holy encounter, an epiphany of the divine life.

A PLACE OF GOD'S APPEARANCE

I spoke about God revealing himself to us in weakness, not only a long time ago in the birth of Jesus but also today wherever people are sick, elderly, dependent, and out of control. I also said that we only live our weakness as a place of God's appearance (it was the day of Epiphany!) when we truly believe we have been loved since we were born and will be loved after we have died. If we do not believe this, our weakness easily leads to bitterness and hardened hearts.

—*Sabbatical Journey*

THE DESCENDING WAY

In the gospel, it's quite obvious that Jesus chose the descending way. He chose it not once but over and over again. At each critical moment he deliberately sought the way downwards. Even though, at twelve years of age, he was already listening to the teachers in the Temple and questioning them, he stayed up to his thirtieth year with his parents in the little-respected town of Nazareth, and was submissive to them. Even though Jesus was without sin, he began his public life by joining the ranks of sinners who were being baptised by John in the Jordan. . . .

His many miracles always serve to express his profound compassion with suffering humanity; never are they attempts to call attention to himself. As a rule, he even forbids those he has cured to talk to others about it. And as Jesus' life continues to unfold, he becomes increasingly aware that he has been called to fulfill his vocation in suffering and death. In all of this, it becomes plain to us that God has willed to show his love for the world by descending more and more deeply into human frailty. In the four accounts of Jesus' life and death you can see very clearly that the more conscious he becomes of the mission entrusted to him by the Father, the more he realizes that that mission will make him poorer and poorer. He has been sent not only to console poor people, but also to give this consolation as one of them himself.

—Letters to Marc about Jesus

THE HUMILITY OF BAPTISM

Jesus, who is without sin, stands in line with sinners waiting to be baptized by John. As Jesus starts his ministry, he chooses to enter into solidarity with sinful humanity. "John tried to dissuade him with the words 'It is I who need baptism from you, and yet you come to me.' But Jesus replied, 'Leave it like this for the time being; it is fitting that we should, in this way, do all that uprightness demands'" (Matthew 3:14–15).

Here we see how Jesus clearly chooses the way of humility. He does not appear with great fanfare as a powerful saviour, announcing a new order. On the contrary, he comes quietly, with the many sinners who are receiving a baptism of repentance. His choice is affirmed by the voice from heaven: "This is my Son, the Beloved, my favour rests on him" (Matthew 3:17). . . .

It is hard to believe that God would reveal his divine presence to us in the self-emptying, humble way of the man from Nazareth. So much in me seeks influence, power, success, and popularity. But the way of Jesus is the way of hiddenness, powerlessness, and littleness. It does not seem a very appealing way. Yet when I enter into true, deep communion with Jesus I will find that it is this small way that leads to real peace and joy.

At this feast of the Lord's baptism, I pray for the courage to choose the small way and to keep choosing it.

—*The Road to Daybreak*

SPIRITUAL DISCOVERIES

The Gospel told the story about Andrew and another disciple of John who followed Jesus. Jesus said: "What are you looking for?" They said: "Rabbi, where do you live?" When Jesus said: "Come and see," they stayed with him. Later, Andrew shared what they had seen and heard with his brother Simon, and so Simon came to Jesus. This story offers three important verbs to reflect upon: to look for, to stay, and to share. When we search for God, stay with him, and share what we have seen with others, we become aware of the unique way that Jesus calls us. A vocation is not a privilege of priests and sisters. Every human being is called by Jesus in a unique way. But we have to be looking for God, we have to be willing to spend time with him, and we must allow others to become part of our spiritual discoveries.

—*¡Gracias!*

THE MIRACLE OF LOVE

Jesus is the revelation of God's unending, unconditional love for us human beings. Everything that Jesus has done, said and undergone is meant to show us that the love we most long for is given to us by

God, not because we've deserved it, but because God is a God of love.

Jesus has come among us to make that divine love visible and to offer it to us. In his conversation with Nicodemus he says: ". . . this is how God loved the world: he gave his only Son. . . . God sent his Son into the world not to judge the world, but so that through him the world might be saved." In these words the meaning of the Incarnation is summed up. God has become human—that is, God-with-us—in order to show us that the anxious concern for recognition and the violence among us spring from a lack of faith in the love of God. If we had a firm faith in God's unconditional love for us, it would no longer be necessary to be always on the lookout for ways of being admired by people, and we would need, even less, to obtain from people by force what God desires to give us so abundantly.

—Letters to Marc about Jesus

THE MIRACLE OF ABUNDANCE

One of the most moving stories about gratitude is the story of the multiplication of bread as told by the evangelist John (6:5–15). When Jesus saw the hungry crowds and wondered where to buy some bread for the people to eat, Andrew said: "There is a small boy here with five barley loaves and two fish; but what is that for so many?" Andrew's word powerfully summarizes our attitude as fearful people. The needs are enormous, the reserves very small, so what can we do? The implication of this attitude is clearly: let us hold on to the little we have so that we at least survive. But "Jesus took the loaves, gave thanks, and gave them out to all who were sitting ready; he then did the same with the fish, giving out as much as was wanted." This radical shift of vision, from looking at the loaves and fishes as scarce products which need to be hoarded, to seeing them as precious gifts from God which ask to be gratefully shared, is the movement from wreaking death to bringing forth life, the movement from fear to love. When the story ends, with the glorious statement that "the disciples filled twelve hampers with scraps left over from the meal of five barley loaves," there is no doubt left that God's house is a house of abundance, not scarcity.

—*In the House of the Lord*

A MOVEMENT FROM THE WOMB OF GOD

There is a beautiful expression in the Gospels that appears only twelve times and is used exclusively in reference to Jesus or his Father. That expression is "to be moved with compassion." The Greek verb *splangchnizoma* reveals to us the deep and powerful meaning of this expression. The *splangchna* are the entrails of the body, or as we might say today, the guts. They are the place where our most intimate and intense emotions are located. They are the centre from which both passionate love and passionate hate grow. When the Gospels speak about Jesus' compassion as his being moved in the entrails, they are expressing something very deep and mysterious. The compassion Jesus felt was obviously quite different from superficial or passing feelings of sorrow or sympathy. Rather, it extended to the most vulnerable part of his being. It is related to the Hebrew word for compassion, *rachamim*, which refers to the womb of Yahweh. Indeed, compassion is such a deep, central, and powerful emotion in Jesus that it can only be described as a movement of the womb of God. There, all the divine tenderness and gentleness lies hidden. There, God is father and mother, brother and sister, son and daughter. There, all feelings, emotions, and passions are one in divine love. When Jesus was moved to compassion, the source of all life trembled, the ground of all love burst open, and the abyss of God's immense, inexhaustible, and unfathomable tenderness revealed itself.

—*Compassion*

UNFATHOMABLE TREASURE

Why must we go out to the far ends of the world to preach the Gospel of Jesus when people do not have to know Jesus in order to enter the house of God? We must go out because we want to share with all people the abundant love and hope, joy and peace that Jesus brought to us. We want to "proclaim the unfathomable treasure of Christ" and "throw light on the inner workings of the mystery kept hidden through all ages in God, the creator of everything" (Ephesians 3:8–9).

What we have received is so beautiful and so rich that we cannot hold it for ourselves but feel compelled to bring it to every human being we meet.

—Bread for the Journey

THE INTIMACY OF HEALING

Out of his solitude Jesus reached out his caring hand to the people in need. In the lonely place his care grew strong and mature. And from there he entered into a healing closeness with his fellow human beings.

Jesus indeed cared. Being pragmatists we say: "That is obvious: he fed the hungry, made the blind see, the deaf hear, the crippled walk and the dead live. He indeed cared." But by being surprised by all the remarkable things he did, we forget that Jesus did not give food to the many without having received some loaves and fishes from a stranger in the crowd; that he did not return the boy of Nain to his widowed mother without having felt her sorrow, that he did not raise Lazarus from the grave without tears and a sigh of distress that came straight from the heart. What we see, and like to see, is cure and change. But what we do not see and do not want to see is care, the participation in the pain, the solidarity in suffering, the sharing in the experience of brokenness. And still, cure without care is as dehumanising as a gift given with a cold heart.

—Out of Solitude

Feasts of Epiphany

ANTHONY OF EGYPT, Hermit, Abbot, 356
(17 January)

St. Anthony, the "father of monks," is the best guide in our attempt to understand the role of solitude in ministry. Born around 251, Anthony was the son of Egyptian peasants. When he was about eighteen years old he heard in church the Gospel words, "Go and sell what you own and give the money to the poor . . . then come and follow me" (Matthew 19:21). Anthony realised that these words were meant for him personally. After a period of living as a poor labourer at the edge of his village, he withdrew into the desert, where for twenty years he lived in complete solitude. During these years Anthony experienced a terrible trial. The shell of his superficial securities was cracked and the abyss of iniquity was opened to him. But he came out of this trial victoriously—not because of his own willpower or ascetic exploits, but because of his unconditional surrender to the Lordship of Jesus Christ. When he emerged from his solitude, people recognised in him the qualities of an authentic "healthy" man, whole in body, mind, and soul. They flocked to him for healing, comfort, and direction. In his old age, Anthony retired to an even deeper solitude to be totally absorbed in direct communion with God. He died in the year 356, when he was about one hundred and six years old.

The story of St. Anthony, as told by St. Athanasius, shows that we must be made aware of the call to let our false, compulsive self be transformed into the new self of Jesus Christ. It also shows that solitude is the furnace in which this transformation takes place. Finally, it reveals that it is from this transformed or converted self that real ministry flows.

—The Way of the Heart

OCTAVE OF PRAYER FOR CHRISTIAN UNITY
(18–25 January)

The Church is one body. Paul writes: "We were baptised into one body in a single Spirit" (1 Corinthians 12:13). But this one body has many parts. As Paul says, "If they were all the same part, how could it be a body? As it is, the parts are many but the body is one" (1 Corinthians 12:19). Not everyone can be everything. Often we expect one member of the body to fulfil a task that belongs to others. But the hand cannot be asked to see nor the eye to hear.

Together we are Christ's body, each of us with a part to play in the whole (see 1 Corinthians 12:27). Let's be grateful for our limited but real part in the body.

—Bread for the Journey

When we have been wounded by the Church, our temptation is to reject it. But when we reject the Church it becomes very hard for us to keep in touch with the living Christ. When we say: "I love Jesus, but I hate the Church," we end up losing not only the Church but Jesus too. The challenge is to forgive the Church. This challenge is especially great because the Church seldom asks us for forgiveness, at least not officially. But the Church as an often fallible human organisation needs our forgiveness, while the Church as the living Christ among us continues to offer us forgiveness.

It is important to think about the Church not as "over there" but as a community of struggling, weak people of whom we are part and in whom we meet our Lord and Redeemer.

—Bread for the Journey

FRANCIS DE SALES, Bishop of Geneva,
Teacher of the Faith, 1622
BIRTH OF HENRI J.M. NOUWEN, 1932
(24 January)

Today, my fifty-fourth birthday, the text of the first reading of the liturgy in honour of St. Francis de Sales summarizes my feelings succinctly. Paul writes to the Ephesians: "I, who am less than the least of all God's holy people, have been entrusted with this special grace, of proclaiming to the Gentiles the unfathomable treasure of Christ and of throwing light on the inner workings of the mystery kept hidden through all the ages in God, the Creator of everything" (Ephesians 3:8–9).

As I reflect on my life today, I feel indeed like the least of God's holy people. Looking back, I realize that I am still struggling with the same problems I had on the day of my ordination twenty-nine years ago. Notwithstanding my many prayers, my periods of retreat, and the advice from many friends, counsellors, and confessors, very little, if anything, has changed with regard to my search for inner unity and peace. I am still the restless, nervous, intense, distracted, and impulse-driven person I was when I set out on this spiritual journey. At times this obvious lack of inner maturation depresses me as I enter into the "mature" years.

But I have one source of consolation. More than ever I feel the desire to proclaim "the unfathomable riches of Christ" and to throw light "on the inner working of the mystery kept hidden through all the ages in God." This desire has grown in intensity and urgency. I want to speak about the riches of Christ much more than when I was ordained in 1957. I vividly remember that the man who ordained me, Bernard Cardinal Alfrink, had written, on his coat of arms, "Evangelizare Divitias Christi" ("to proclaim the riches of Christ"). Today, when I read these same words in the liturgy, I realize that I have made these words increasingly my own. I really do want to speak loudly and clearly about the great riches of Christ. I want to do it simply, directly, plainly, and with deep personal conviction. Here I feel that something has grown in me. Here I sense that I am not the same person I was twenty-nine years ago.

Maybe an increasing awareness of my sinfulness, as well as an increasing desire to make known the unfathomable riches of Christ, will prevent me from becoming proud, self-righteous, manipulative, and oppressive. I pray today that my sins will make me humble and my call to witness for Christ courageous. Francis de Sales is the best possible example I can have on this day to thank God for my life and to ask for faithfulness to the ministry given to me.

        —*The Road to Daybreak*

Birthdays need to be celebrated. I think it is more important to celebrate a birthday than a successful exam, a promotion, or a victory. Because to celebrate a birthday means to say to someone: "Thank you for being you." Celebrating a birthday is exalting life and being glad for it. On a birthday we do not say: "Thanks for what you did, or said, or accomplished." No, we say: "Thank you for being born and being among us."

        —*Here and Now*

THE CONVERSION OF PAUL
(25 January)

When we think about prayer, we usually regard it as one of the many things we do to live a full and mature Christian life. . . . If we are fervent in our conviction that prayer is important, we might even be willing to give a whole hour to prayer every day, or a whole day every month, or a whole week every year. Thus prayer becomes a part, a very important part, of our life.

But when the apostle Paul speaks about prayer, he uses a very different language. He does not speak about prayer as a part of life, but as all of life. He does not mention prayer as something we should not forget, but claims it is our ongoing concern. He does not exhort his readers to pray once in a while, regularly, or often, but without hesitation admonishes them to pray constantly, unceasingly, without interruption. Paul does not ask us to spend some of every day in prayer. No, Paul is much more radical. He asks us to pray every day and night, in joy and in sorrow, at work and at play, without intermissions or breaks. For Paul, praying is like breathing. It cannot be interrupted without mortal danger.

—*Clowning in Rome*

Do you really want to be converted? Are you willing to be transformed? Or do you keep clutching your old ways of life with one hand while with the other you beg people to help you change?

Conversion is certainly not something you can bring about yourself. It is not a question of willpower. You have to trust the inner voice that shows the way. You know that inner voice. You turn to it often. But after you have heard with clarity what you are asked to do, you start raising questions, fabricating objections, and seeking everyone else's opinion. Thus you become entangled in countless often contradictory thoughts, feelings, and ideas and lose touch with the God in you. And you end up dependent on all the people you have gathered around you.

Only by attending constantly to the inner voice can you be converted to a new life of freedom and joy.

—*The Inner Voice of Love*

TIMOTHY AND TITUS, Companions of Paul
(26 January)

When Jesus speaks about patience, he describes it as the discipline by which God's life-giving presence becomes manifest. . . . The active, strong, and fruitful patience about which Jesus speaks is repeatedly praised by the apostles Paul, Peter, James, and John as the mark of the true disciple. Paul in particular offers us a deep insight into the power of patience. He exhorts his friend Timothy to be patient and gentle (1 Timothy 6:11) and writes to the Christians at Colossae, "You should be clothed in sincere compassion, in kindness and humility, gentleness and patience" (Colossians 3:12). He does not hesitate to offer himself as an example of patience (2 Timothy 3:10) and to see patience as the source of an intimate solidarity between himself and his people. . . . For Paul patience is indeed the discipline of the compassionate life.

—*Compassion*

Once God has touched us in the midst of our struggles and has created in us the burning desire to be for ever united with him, we will find the courage and the confidence to prepare his way and to invite all who share our life to wait with us during this short time for the day of complete joy. With this new courage and new confidence we can strengthen each other with the hopeful words of Paul to Titus:

> . . . God's grace has been revealed, and it has made salvation possible for the whole human race and taught us that what we have to do is to give up everything that does not lead to God, and all our worldly ambitions; we must be self-restrained and live good and religious lives here in this present world, while we are waiting in hope for the blessing which will come with the Appearing of the glory of our great God and Saviour Jesus Christ (Titus 2:11–13).

—*Reaching Out*

THE PRESENTATION OF CHRIST IN THE TEMPLE (CANDLEMAS)
(2 February)

Mary and Joseph took Jesus to Jerusalem "to present him to the Lord" and to offer the Lord the sacrifice of the poor, "a pair of turtledoves or two young pigeons." There in the temple they met two old people, Simeon and Anna, who sensed the sacredness of the moment and spoke words about the child that astounded his parents.

Every time I try to meditate on a sacred event such as this, I find myself tempted to think about it in an intellectual way. But today I realized more strongly than ever before that I simply have to be there. I have to travel with Mary and Joseph to Jerusalem, walk with them on the busy temple square, join the thousands of simple people in offering their simple gifts, feel somewhat lost and awed by it all, and listen to two unknown old people who have something to say, something that sounds very strange and even frightening. Why do I want more? Why do I want to add a comment to it all? It is as if I want to keep some distance. But the story is so simple, so crystal clear, so unpretentious. I do not have to do anything with it. I do not have to explain or examine these events. I simply have to step into them and allow them to surround me, to leave me silent. I do not have to master or capture them. I have only to be carried by them to places where I am as small, quiet, and inconspicuous as the child of Mary and Joseph.

Something of that happened to me as I went through the day. I kept seeing Simeon and Anna; and instead of disregarding them as two pious old church mice who disturbed me with their aggressive predictions, I sat down for a while and allowed them to speak and me to listen. I heard Simeon and Anna many times over during the day, and I suddenly realized that they have been trying to speak to me for a long time.

—*¡Gracias!*

Together with [Rembrandt's] unfinished painting *Simeon and the Child Jesus*, the Prodigal Son shows the painter's perception of his aged self—a perception in which physical blindness and a deep inner seeing are intimately connected. The way in which the old Simeon holds the vulnerable child and the way in which the old father embraces his exhausted son reveal an inner vision that reminds one of Jesus' words to his disciples: "Blessed are the eyes that see what you see." Both Simeon and the father of the returning son carry *within* themselves that mysterious light by which they see. It is an inner light, deeply hidden, but radiating an all-pervasive tender beauty.

—*The Return of the Prodigal Son*

In my [dying] friend's presence I felt no desire to ask questions about the past or to speculate about the future. We were just together without fear, without guilt or shame, without worries. In that emptiness, God's unconditional love could be sensed and we could say what the old Simeon said when he took the Christ child in his arms: "Now, Master, you can let your servant go in peace as you have promised." There, in the midst of the dreadful emptiness, was complete trust, complete peace, and complete joy. Death no longer was the enemy. Love was victorious.

—*The Return of the Prodigal Son*

OUR LADY OF LOURDES
(11 February)

There are very few pilgrims at this time of year. I am here alone. After the long, tiring night on the train, I arrived at "the little convent" of the Sisters of the Immaculate Conception at 7:30 a.m. I slept, went to the grotto where Mary appeared to Bernadette, celebrated the Eucharist of the Epiphany in the basilica, and prayed.

Why am I here? To give my life to Jesus. To make Jesus the very center of my existence. But how is this to come about? Mary is here to show me, Mary is here to be my gentle counsellor, to take me by the hand and let me enter into full communion with her son.

I am afraid, but Mary is here and tells me to trust. I realize that I can make Jesus the heart of my heart only when I ask Mary to show me how. She is the mother of Jesus. In her, God interrupted history and started to make everything new. And so I too have to put myself under her protection. . . . I simply want to be very close to her who spoke to Bernadette in the grotto. I trust that she will open my heart for a new encounter with Jesus.

—*Jesus and Mary*

THE CHAIR OF PETER THE APOSTLE
(22 February)

When you can say to Jesus, "You are the Messiah, the Son of the living God," Jesus can say to you, "You are the rock on whom I will build my church." There is a mutuality of recognition and a mutuality of truth here. When we acknowledge that God has come among us through the Messiah—his anointed one—to free us from our captivity, God can point to our solid core and make us the foundation for a community of faith.

Our "rock" quality will be revealed to us when we confess our need for salvation and healing. We can become community builders when we are humble enough to see our dependence on God.

It is sad that the dialogue between Jesus and Simon Peter has, in my church, been almost exclusively used to explain the role of the papacy. By doing so, it seems to me that we miss seeing that this exchange is for all of us. We all have to confess our need for salvation, and we all have to accept our solid centre.

And the keys of the kingdom? They too belong first to all who confess Jesus as their Christ and thus come to belong to a community of faith in which our binding and unbinding happen in the Name of God. When indeed the body of Christ, formed by believers, makes decisions about its members, these are Kingdom decisions. That is what Jesus refers to when he says, "Whatever you bind on earth will be bound in heaven, and whatever you loose on earth will be loosed in heaven" (Matthew 16:19).

These thoughts came to my mind on this Feast of the Chair of St. Peter, as we were gathering around the table with several people who had left the Catholic Church because they saw it as too authoritarian. More than ever it is important to realize that the Church is not simply "over there," where the bishops are or where the Pope is, but "right here," where we are around the table of the Lord.

—Sabbatical Journey

SHROVE TUESDAY

Dear Lord Jesus,

Tomorrow the Lenten season begins. It is a time to be with you in a special way, a time to pray, to fast, and thus to follow you on your way to Jerusalem, to Golgotha, and to the final victory over death.

I am still so divided. I truly want to follow you, but I also want to follow my own desires and lend an ear to the voices that speak about prestige, success, human respect, pleasure, power, and influence. Help me to become deaf to these voices and more attentive to your voice, which calls me to choose the narrow road to life.

I know that Lent is going to be a very hard time for me. The choice for your way has to be made every moment of my life. I have to choose thoughts that are your thoughts, words that are your words, and actions that are your actions. There are no times or places without choices. And I know how deeply I resist choosing you.

Please, Lord, be with me at every moment and in every place. Give me the strength and the courage to live this season faithfully, so that, when Easter comes, I will be able to taste with joy the new life which you have prepared for me.

Amen.

—*The Road to Daybreak*

Note: Also known as "Fat Tuesday" or "Mardi Gras," Shrove Tuesday is the day of preparation for Lent. The name "shrove" is rumored to derive from the word "shrive" or confess. It takes place on the Tuesday before Ash Wednesday (the first day of Lent).

Lent

Season of Repentance

Lent

Henri Nouwen once described Lent as the season during which winter and spring struggle with each other for dominance. I think this is an appropriate image because during this time of year the darkness and light within each of us can become locked in conflict. We are called not only to examine the integrity of our own motives but to work courageously for justice in the world around us.

Lent, which means springtime, is traditionally a six-week period of abstinence and repentance in preparation for Easter. As the buds open on trees and the days lengthen, this is a spiritual season which calls for greater openness to the word of God and a conversion in every area of our lives. It is a time to face the darkness within and expose it to the light.

Lent is the season to confront our demons and expel them.

Henri Nouwen was troubled by demons throughout his life. He knew that his temptation was actually to be so obsessed by his sins and failings that he could become stuck in a paralysing guilt. This led him to introspection. Guilt became an idol and therefore a form of pride. Lent, he concluded, was the time to break down this idol and direct his eyes to a loving God.

Nouwen is especially associated with this season because of his book, *The Return of the Prodigal Son*, which has been used by many groups for study at this time of the year. When we met, he talked a lot about the effect the painting had had on him, especially the embrace of the father and son. "It evoked something very deep in me," he explained. "I was very tired, very frazzled and felt very fragmented interiorly. When I saw this experience of homecoming, belonging and safety, this embrace of love, I suddenly said: 'This is what I most desire to be: to be welcomed home so fully and so intimately. It became, not only a summary of my whole life, but a vocation to something new.'"

I remember asking him if there was a danger that he was merely projecting his own needs onto the canvas and hoping it would reflect what he wanted to see. "I don't think it's a danger," he replied. "I think a painting allows me to project. But it also allows me to come in touch with things in myself. I'm not suggesting Rembrandt expected anybody to use the painting the way I did but I have that wonderful freedom to look at a painting and let it become an icon, bringing me in touch with my deepest self."

After the interview, I drove him into the rain-soaked English countryside where we squelched about in the mud en route to his rural speaking engagement. Holding our trousers above our ankles, we laughed as we sloshed our way across a miry field. There was no red carpet for this bestselling writer who struck me as a humble mystic. In the following sequences, Nouwen wrestles honestly with his failings, trusting explicitly in the merciful love of a God whose heart is entirely void of self-seeking. This divine image of compassion and forgiveness encourages Nouwen to let go of his attachments and reach out to God.

ASH WEDNESDAY

I am certainly not ready for Lent yet. Christmas seems just behind us, and Lent seems an unwelcome guest. I could have used a few more weeks to get ready for this season of repentance, prayer, and preparation for the death and resurrection of Jesus. . . .

I spoke about how Jesus stressed the hidden life. Whether we give alms, pray, or fast, we are to do it in a hidden way, not to be praised by people but to enter into closer communion with God. Lent is a time of returning to God. It is a time to confess how we keep looking for joy, peace and satisfaction in the many people and things surrounding us, without really finding what we desire. Only God can give us what we want. So we must be reconciled with God, as Paul says, and let that reconciliation be the basis of our relationships with others. Lent is a time of refocusing, of re-entering the place of truth, of reclaiming our true identity.

—*Sabbatical Journey*

LITTLE DEATHS

O Lord, it is a great grace that I can be in this monastery during Lent. How often have I lived through these weeks without paying much attention to penance, fasting and prayer? How often have I missed the spiritual fruits of this season without even being aware of it? But how can I ever really celebrate Easter without observing Lent? How can I rejoice fully in your resurrection when I have avoided participating in your death?

Yes, Lord, I have to die—with you, through you, and in you— and thus become ready to recognize you when you appear to me in your resurrection. There is so much in me that needs to die: false attachments, greed and anger, impatience and stinginess. O Lord, I am self-centred, concerned about myself, my career, my future, my name and fame. Often I even feel that I use you for my own advantage. How preposterous, how sacrilegious, how sad! But yes, Lord, I know it is true. I know that often I have spoken about you, written about you, and acted in your name for my own glory and for my own success. Your name has not led me to persecution, oppression, or rejection. Your name has brought me rewards! I see clearly now how little I have died with you, really gone your way and been faithful to it. O Lord, make this Lenten season different from the other ones. Let me find you again. Amen.

—*A Cry for Mercy*

DISTANT ADDICTIONS

"Addiction" might be the best word to explain the lostness that so deeply permeates contemporary society. Our addictions make us cling to what the world proclaims as the keys to self-fulfilment: accumulation of wealth and power; attainment of status and admiration; lavish consumption of food and drink; and sexual gratification without distinguishing between lust and love. These addictions create expectations that cannot but fail to satisfy our deepest needs. As long as we live within the world's delusions, our addictions condemn us to futile quests in "the distant country," leaving us to face an endless series of disillusionments while our sense of self remains unfulfilled. In these days of increasing addictions, we have wandered far away from our Father's home. The addicted life can aptly be designated a life lived in "a distant country." It is from there that our cry for deliverance rises up.

I am the prodigal son every time I search for unconditional love where it cannot be found. Why do I keep ignoring the place of true love and persist in looking for it elsewhere? Why do I keep leaving home where I am called a child of God, the Beloved of my Father? I am constantly surprised at how I keep taking the gifts God had given me—my health, my intellectual and emotional gifts—and keep using them to impress people, receive affirmation and praise, and compete for rewards, instead of developing them for the glory of God.

—*The Return of the Prodigal Son*

TESTING TIMES

Jesus is the compassionate God who comes so close to us in our weakness that we can turn to him without fear. The Letter to the Hebrews puts it in incomparably profound words: "He has been put to the test in exactly the same way as ourselves, apart from sin. Let us, then, have no fear in approaching the throne of grace to receive mercy and to find grace when we are in need of help."

I hope that you can grasp something of all this and take it to heart. In the end, I think it is only through prayer that you can come to understand it. When you stand before God, vulnerable as you are, and let him see all there is of you, you will begin gradually to experience for yourself what it means that God has sent Jesus to be, in all things, God-with-you. Then you will begin to know that, by becoming a human being in Jesus, God is offering you his divine life. Then you can ask yourself in a new way how you wish to conduct your own life.

—*Letters to Marc about Jesus*

POWERFUL TEMPTATIONS

Too often I looked at being relevant, popular, and powerful as ingredients of an effective ministry. The truth, however, is that these are not vocations but temptations. Jesus asks, "Do you love me?" Jesus sends us out to be shepherds, and Jesus promises a life in which we increasingly have to stretch out our hands and be led to places where we would rather not go. He asks us to move from a concern for relevance to a life of prayer, from worries about popularity to communal and mutual ministry, and from a leadership built on power to a leadership in which we critically discern where God is leading us and our people.

—*In the Name of Jesus*

NO HIDING PLACE

When God asked Adam, "Where are you?" Adam answered, "I was hiding" (Genesis 3:9–10). He confessed his true condition. This confession opened him to God. When we pray, we come out of our shelters and not only see our own nakedness but also see that there is no enemy to hide from, only a friend who likes nothing better than to clothe us with a new coat. Certainly praying takes some admissions. It requires the humble recognition of our own condition as broken human beings. However, prayer does not lead us to shame, guilt, or despair, but rather to the joyful discovery that we are only human and that God is truly God.

If we cling tightly to our own weakness, our faults, shortcomings, and our twisted past, to all the events, facts, and situations which we would prefer to cut out of our own history, we are only hiding behind a hedge through which everyone can see. What we have done is to narrow our world to a small hiding place where we try to conceal ourselves, suspecting rather pitifully that everyone has seen us all along.

—*With Open Hands*

SACRAMENTAL ENCOUNTER

Confession and forgiveness are the concrete forms in which we sinful people love one another. Often I have the impression that priests and ministers are the least-confessing people in the Christian community. The sacrament of Confession has often become a way to keep our own vulnerability hidden from our community. Sins are mentioned and ritual words of forgiveness are spoken, but seldom does a real encounter take place in which the reconciling and healing presence of Jesus can be experienced. There is so much fear, so much distance, so much generalization and so little real listening, speaking, and absolving, that not much true sacramentality can be expected.

—*In the Name of Jesus*

FORGIVING YOURSELF

Maybe someone will say to you, "You have to forgive yourself." But that isn't possible. What is possible is to open your hands without fear, so that the One who loves you can blow your sins away. Then the coins you considered indispensable for your life prove to be little more than light dust which a soft breeze will whirl away, leaving only a grin or a chuckle behind. Then you feel a bit of new freedom, and praying becomes a joy, a spontaneous reaction to the world, and the people around you. Praying then becomes effortless, inspired and lively, or peaceful and quiet. When you recognize the festive and the still moments as moments of prayer, then you gradually realize that to pray is to live.

    —With Open Hands

STEPPING OVER RESENTMENTS

It is through constant forgiveness that we become like the Father. Forgiveness from the heart is very, very difficult. It is next to impossible. Jesus said to his disciples: "When your brother wrongs you seven times a day and seven times comes back to you and says, 'I am sorry,' you must forgive him."

I have often said, "I forgive you," but even as I said these words my heart remained angry or resentful. I still wanted to hear the story that tells me that I was right after all; I still wanted to hear apologies and excuses; I still wanted the satisfaction of receiving some praise in return—if only the praise for being so forgiving!

But God's forgiveness is unconditional; it comes from a heart that does not demand anything for itself, a heart that is completely empty of self-seeking. It is this divine forgiveness that I have to practice in my daily life. It calls me to keep stepping over all my arguments that say forgiveness is unwise, unhealthy, and impractical. It challenges me to step over all my needs for gratitude and compliments. Finally, it demands of me that I step over that wounded part of my heart that feels hurt and wronged and that wants to stay in control and put a few conditions between me and the one whom I am asked to forgive.

This "stepping over" is the authentic discipline of forgiveness. Maybe it is more "climbing over" than "stepping over." Often I have to climb over the wall of arguments and angry feelings that I have erected between myself and all those whom I love but who so often do not return that love. It is a wall of fear of being used or hurt again. It is a wall of pride, and the desire to stay in control. But every time that I can step or climb over that wall, I enter into the house where the Father dwells, and there touch my neighbour with genuine compassionate love.

—*The Return of the Prodigal Son*

WATER OF ETERNITY

Dear Lord, thank you for the beginning of spring. In the midst of Lent I am made aware that Easter is coming again: the days are becoming longer, the snow is withdrawing, the sun is bringing new warmth, and a bird is singing. Yesterday, during the night prayers, a cat was crying! Indeed, spring announces itself. And tonight, O Lord, I heard you speak to the Samaritan woman. You said: "Anyone who drinks the water that I shall give you will never be thirsty again; the water that I shall give will turn into a spring inside him, welling up to eternal life." What words! They are worth many hours, days, and weeks of reflection. I will carry them with me in my preparation for Easter. The water that you give turns into a spring. Therefore, I do not have to be stingy with your gift, O Lord. I can freely let the water come from my center and let anyone who desires drink from it. Perhaps I will even see this spring in myself when others come to it to quench their thirst. So often, Lord, I doubt that there is a spring in me; so often I am afraid that it has dried up or has been filled with sand. But others keep believing in the spring in me even when I do not.

Let the spring of this year and the spring of water in me give me joy, O Lord, my hope and my Redeemer. Amen.

—*A Cry for Mercy*

TEARS OF COMPASSION

It might sound strange to consider grief a way to compassion. But it is. Grief asks me to allow the sins of the world—my own included—

to pierce my heart and make me shed tears, many tears, for them. There is no compassion without many tears. If they can't be tears that stream from my eyes, they have to be at least tears that well up from my heart. When I consider the immense waywardness of God's children, our lust, our greed, our violence, our anger, our resentment, and when I look at them through the eyes of God's heart, I cannot but weep and cry out in grief:

> Look, my soul, at the way one human being tries to inflict as much pain on another as possible; look at these people plotting to bring harm to their fellows; look at these parents molesting their children; look at this landowner exploiting his workers; look at the violated women, the misused men, the abandoned children. Look, my soul, at the world; see the concentration camps, the prisons, the nursing homes, the hospitals, and hear the cries of the poor.

This grieving is praying. There are so few mourners left in this world. But grief is the discipline of the heart that sees the sin of the world, and knows itself to be the sorrowful price of freedom without which love cannot blossom. I am beginning to see that much of praying is grieving. This grief is so deep not just because the human sin is so great, but also—and more so—because the divine love is so boundless. To become like the Father whose only authority is compassion, I have to shed countless tears and so prepare my heart to receive anyone, whatever their journey has been, and forgive them from that heart.

—*The Return of the Prodigal Son*

THE MYSTERY OF DARKNESS

O Lord, this holy season of Lent is passing quickly. I entered into it with fear, but also with great expectations. I hoped for a great breakthrough, a powerful conversion, a real change of heart; I wanted Easter to be a day so full of light that not even a trace of darkness would be left in my soul. But I know that you do not come to your people with thunder and lightning. Even St. Paul and St. Francis journeyed through much darkness before they could see your light. Let me be thankful for your gentle way. I know you are at work. I know you will not leave me alone. I know you are quickening me for Easter—but in a way fitting to my own history and my own temperament.

I pray that these last three weeks, in which you invite me to enter more fully into the mystery of your passion, will bring me a greater desire to follow you on the way that you create for me and to accept the cross that you give to me. Let me die to the desire to choose my own way and select my own cross. You do not want to make me a hero but a servant who loves you.

Be with me tomorrow and in the days to come, and let me experience your gentle presence. Amen.

—*A Cry for Mercy*

INTIMATE ABSENCE

Precisely where we feel most present to each other we experience deeply the absence of those we love. And precisely at moments of great loss we can discover a new sense of closeness and intimacy. This is also what the Eucharist is about. We announce the presence of Christ among us until he comes again! There is both presence and absence, closeness and distance, an experience of at-homeness on the way home.

I was struck again by the paradox that loving someone deeply means opening yourself to the pain of her or his absence. Lent is a time to get in touch with our experience of absence, emptiness, unfulfilment, so that in the midst of our overcrowded lives we can remind ourselves that we are still waiting for the One who has promised to fulfil our deepest desires.

—*Sabbatical Journey*

REBELLION OR RESTORATION?

One of the greatest challenges of the spiritual life is to receive God's forgiveness. There is something in us humans that keeps us clinging to our sins and prevents us from letting God erase our past and offer us a completely new beginning. Sometimes it even seems as though I want to prove to God that my darkness is too great to overcome. While God wants to restore me to the full dignity of sonship, I keep insisting that I will settle for being a hired servant. But do I truly want to be restored to the full responsibility of the son? Do I truly want to be so totally forgiven that a completely new way of living becomes possible? Do I trust myself and such a radical reclamation? Do I want to break away from my deep-rooted rebellion against God and surrender myself so absolutely to God's love that a new person can emerge? Receiving forgiveness requires a total willingness to let God be God and do all the healing, restoring, and renewing. As long as I want to do even a part of that myself, I end up with partial solutions, such as becoming a hired servant. As a hired servant, I can still keep my distance, still revolt, reject, strike, run away, or complain about my pay. As the beloved son, I have to claim my full dignity and begin preparing myself to become the father.

—*The Return of the Prodigal Son*

THE EMBRACE OF LOVE

As Father, the only authority he claims for himself is the authority of compassion. That authority comes from letting the sins of his children pierce his heart. There is no lust, greed, anger, resentment, jealousy, or vengeance in his lost children that has not caused immense grief to his heart. The grief is so deep because the heart is so pure. From the deep inner place where love embraces all human grief, the Father reaches out to his children. The touch of his hands, radiating inner light, seeks only to heal.

Here is the God I want to believe in: a Father who, from the beginning of creation, has stretched out his arms in merciful blessing, never forcing himself on anyone, but always waiting; never letting his arms drop down in despair, but always hoping that his children will return so that he can speak words of love to them and let his tired arms rest on their shoulders. His only desire is to bless.

—*The Return of the Prodigal Son*

Feasts of Lent

DAVID, Bishop of Menevia, Patron of Wales, c. 601
(1 March)

The Church is a very human organisation but also the garden of God's grace. It is a place where great sanctity keeps blooming. Saints are people who make the living Christ visible to us in a special way. Some saints have given their lives in the service of Christ and his Church; others have spoken and written words that keep nurturing us; some have lived heroically in difficult situations; others have remained hidden in quiet lives of prayer and meditation; some were prophetic voices calling for renewal; others were spiritual strategists setting up large organisations or networks of people; some were healthy and strong; others were quite sick, and often anxious and insecure.

But all of them in their own ways lived in the Church as in a garden where they heard the voice calling them the Beloved and where they found the courage to make Jesus the centre of their lives.

—*Bread for the Journey*

PATRICK, Bishop of Armagh, Missionary,
Patron of Ireland, c. 460
(17 March)

There are more people on this planet outside the Church than inside it. Millions have been baptised, millions have not. Millions participate in the celebration of the Lord's Supper, but millions do not.

The Church as the body of Christ, as Christ living in the world, has a larger mission than to support, nurture, and guide its own members. It is also called to be a witness to the love of God made visible in Jesus. Before his death Jesus prayed for his followers, 'As you sent me into the world, I have sent them into the world' (John 17:18). Part of the essence of being the Church is being a living witness for Christ in the world.

—Bread for the Journey

JOSEPH OF NAZARETH
(19 March)

Often the family of Jesus is portrayed as the model for all families. But a closer look at the way Joseph, Mary, and Jesus lived together evokes little desire for imitation. Indeed, Joseph was a very decent man. He didn't want to give his pregnant girlfriend a bad reputation, and after a reassuring dream, he married her. But was it a happy life? When Jesus was twelve they lost him in the crowd, and when they found him, after three days of anxiously looking, their question: 'Why did you do this to us?' was answered with something close to a reproach: 'Did you not know that I must be in my Father's house' (Luke 2:49)? This response, 'But didn't you know I have more important things to do than pay attention to you,' is hardly consoling.

. . . In this time of broken families, of separation, and divorce, of children with only one parent, and of mothers and fathers in great anxiety about their suicidal or drug-using kids, the seemingly quite dysfunctional family of Jesus may offer us some solace! It is clear to me that Jesus is quite ambivalent, if not negative, about so-called family values such as family harmony, filial affection, staying together at all costs. I wonder if our church's elevation of celibacy, especially for those who want to serve God, does not have its roots in the quite disturbing situation of Jesus' own family.

But Joseph is a saint! He lived it all in a great hiddenness. Ignored by the Gospel writers, and by the early church, he emerges today as a man trusting in God even when there was hardly anything for him to hold on to.

—Sabbatical Journey

Note: The feast of Joseph the Worker is celebrated on 1 May.

THE ANNUNCIATION OF THE LORD
(25 March)

My meditation on the Annunciation brought me real peace and joy, while reflections on other mysteries could not keep me focused. As I tried to simply be with Mary and listen to her words, "You see before you the Lord's servant; let it happen to me as you have said" (Luke 1:38), I discovered a restful peace. Instead of thinking about these words and trying to understand them, I just listened to them being spoken for me.

Mary is so open, so free, so trusting. She is completely willing to hear words that go far beyond her own comprehension. She knows that the words spoken to her by the angel come from God. She seeks clarification, but she does not question their authority. She senses that the message of Gabriel will radically interrupt her life, and she is afraid, but she does not withdraw. When she hears the words "You will bear a son . . . he will be called the son of the Most High," she asks, "But how can this come about, since I have no knowledge of this man?" Then she hears what no other human being ever heard: "The Holy Spirit will come upon you and the power of the Most High will cover you with its shadow." She responded with a complete surrender and thus became not only the mother of Jesus but also the mother of all who believe in him. " . . . let it happen to me as you have said" (Luke 1:34–35, 38).

I keep listening to these words as words that summarize the deepest possible response to God's loving action within us. God wants to let the Holy Spirit guide our lives, but are we prepared to let it happen? Just being with Mary and the angel and hearing their words—words which changed the course of history—bring me peace and rest.

—*The Road to Daybreak*

Holy Week

Season of Passion

Holy Week

Lent reaches its climax during Holy Week, itself a journey within a journey. The pace of the liturgical year seems to slow down until, in the paschal triduum, from Maundy Thursday to the Easter Vigil, we recall the stages of Christ's passing from this world. It is a solemn passage through loneliness, betrayal, injustice and brutal suffering. It is a movement from life to death.

Henri Nouwen believed his ministry was to witness to God's redemptive love with his whole being. He told me that he tried to adopt the attitude of acknowledging that "I am the one who needs to be redeemed. I want to share the struggles that I'm living to see how the Gospel responds." He said it was a way of laying down his life for his friends. He looked me straight in the eye and explained: "Jesus says the Good Shepherd lays down his life for his friends."

These words were brought home to me during the Holy Week I spent in New York while researching a book on the first registered victim of September 11, 2001, Father Mychal Judge, a priest who had laid down his life for others. Heroic virtue, I was told, had been demonstrated by Father Mike that morning in a way that redeemed the evil of the event itself. He had been the victim who saved. In the chill of Good Friday I stood solemnly at Ground Zero, where the birds no longer sing, and imagined the ministry of this smiling friar who had cared unstintingly for others while struggling with his own internal conflict and pain. Father Mike had been inspired by the life and writings of Henri Nouwen.

Holy Week means accompanying Christ on his final journey, bearing our own crosses in trusting silence.

By embracing his own loneliness, depression, and struggles in faith, Henri Nouwen, too, trusted that he would find light and hope in the center of his pain. In the world sadness and gladness are always separate, he told me, but in the spiritual life they are all of a piece. "In the world if you're sad, you cannot be glad. If you're glad, you cannot be sad—be happy and forget your troubles. In the spiritual life it's precisely the opposite. You embrace your sadness and trust that, right there, you will find gladness. That's what the cross is all about. I look at the cross, a sign of execution, of pain, of torture, and see it as my hope. The cross is a source of life for me. The cross brings me joy. By embracing the pain, you're speaking about joy. And that's a very, very spiritual thing."

Henri Nouwen made his own journey to the cross each year in a number of different countries. These reflections, from various periods, reveal a pilgrim faithfully following his Lord and Saviour as the drama of Holy Week unfolds.

PALM SUNDAY

Christ on a Donkey, in the Augustiner Museum in Freiburg, is one of the most moving Christ figures I know.

I went to the museum to spend some quiet time with this *Christus auf Palmesel* (Christ on a palm-donkey). This fourteenth-century sculpture originally comes from Niederotweil, a small town close to Breisach on the Rhine. It was made to be pulled on a cart in the Palm Sunday procession. . . .

Christ's long, slender face with a high forehead, inward-looking eyes, long hair, and a small forked beard expresses the mystery of his suffering in a way that holds me spellbound. As he rides into Jerusalem surrounded by people shouting "hosanna," "cutting branches from the trees and spreading them in his path" (Matthew

21:8), Jesus appears completely concentrated on something else. He does not look at the excited crowd. He does not wave. He sees beyond all the noise and movement to what is ahead of him: an agonizing journey of betrayal, torture, crucifixion, and death. His unfocused eyes see what nobody around him can see; his high forehead reflects a knowledge of things to come far beyond anyone's understanding.

There is melancholy, but also peaceful acceptance. There is insight into the fickleness of the human heart, but also immense compassion. There is a deep awareness of the unspeakable pain to be suffered, but also a strong determination to do God's will. Above all, there is love, an endless, deep, and far-reaching love born from an unbreakable intimacy with God and reaching out to all people, wherever they are, were, or will be. There is nothing that he does not fully know. There is nobody whom he does not fully love.

Every time I look at this Christ on a donkey, I am reminded again that I am seen by him with all my sins, guilt, and shame and loved with all his forgiveness, mercy, and compassion.

—*The Road to Daybreak*

HOLY MONDAY

During this Holy Week we are confronted with death more than during any other season of the liturgical year. We are called to meditate not just on death in general or on our own death in particular, but on the death of Jesus Christ who is God and man. We are challenged to look at him dying on a cross and to find there the meaning of our own life and death. What strikes me most in all that is read and said during these days is that Jesus of Nazareth did not die for himself, but for us, and that in following him we too are called to make our death a death for others. What makes you and me Christians is not only our belief that he who was without sin died for our sake on the cross and thus opened for us the way to his heavenly Father, but also that through his death our death is transformed from a totally absurd end of all that gives life its meaning into an event that liberates us and those whom we love.

—*A Letter of Consolation*

Passion is a kind of waiting—waiting for what other people are going to do. Jesus went to Jerusalem to announce the good news to the people of that city. And Jesus knew he was going to put a choice before them: Will you be my disciple, or will you be my executioner? There is no middle ground here. Jesus went to Jerusalem to put people in a situation where they had to say "Yes"or "No." That is the great drama of Jesus' passion: he had to wait upon how people were going to respond. What would they do? Betray him or follow him?

—*The Path of Waiting*

HOLY TUESDAY

Jesus, sitting at table with his disciples, said, "One of you will betray me" (John 13:21). I read this today in the Gospel.

As I look more closely at Jesus' words as they are written in Greek, a better translation would be "One of you will hand me over." The term *paradidomi* means "to give over, to hand over, to give into the hands of" (Romans 8:32).

If we translate Judas's action as "to betray," as applied to Judas, we do not fully express the mystery because Judas is described as being an instrument of God's work. That is why Jesus said, "The Son of Man is going to his fate, as the scriptures say he will, but alas for the man by whom the Son of Man is betrayed [handed over]" (Matthew 26:24).

This moment when Jesus is handed over to those who do with him as they please is a turning point in Jesus' ministry. It is turning from action to passion. After years of teaching, preaching, healing, and moving to wherever he wanted to go, Jesus is handed over to the caprices of his enemies. Things are no longer done *by* him, but *to* him. He is flagellated, crowned with thorns, spat at, laughed at, stripped, and nailed naked to a cross. He is a passive victim, subject to other people's actions. From the moment Jesus is handed over, his passion begins, and through his passion he fulfils his vocation.

It is important for me to realize that Jesus fulfils his mission not by what he does, but by what is done to him. Just as with everyone else, most of my life is determined by what is done to me and thus is passion. And because most of my life is passion, things being done to me, only small parts of my life are determined by what I think, say, or do. I am inclined to protest against this and to want all to be action, originated by me. But the truth is that my passion is a much greater part of my life than my action. Not to recognize this is self-deception and not to embrace my passion with love is self-rejection.

It is good news to know that Jesus is handed over to passion and through his passion accomplishes his divine task on earth. It is good news for a world passionately searching for wholeness.

Jesus' words to Peter remind me that Jesus is handed over to passion and through his passion accomplishes his divine task on earth. It is good news for a world passionately searching for wholeness.

Jesus' words to Peter remind me that Jesus' transition from action to passion must also be ours if we want to follow his way. He says, "When you were young you put on your own belt and walked where you liked; but when you grow old you will stretch out your hands, and somebody else will take you where you would rather not go" (John 21:18).

I, too, have to let myself be "handed over" and thus fulfill my vocation.

—*The Road to Daybreak*

People who live close together can be sources of great sorrow for each other. When Jesus chose his twelve apostles, Judas was one of them. Judas is called a traitor. A traitor, according to the literal meaning of the Greek word for "betraying," is someone who hands the other over to suffering.

The truth is that we all have something of the traitor in us because each of us hands our fellow human beings over to suffering somehow, somewhere, mostly without intending or even knowing it. Many children, even grown-up children, can experience deep anger toward their parents for having protected them too much or too little. When we are willing to confess that we often hand those we love over to suffering, even against our best intentions, we will be more ready to forgive those who, mostly against their will, are the causes of our pain.

—*Bread for the Journey*

HOLY WEDNESDAY

Judas betrayed Jesus. Peter denied him. Both were lost children. Judas, no longer able to hold on to the truth that he remained God's child, hung [sic] himself. In terms of the prodigal son, he sold the sword of his sonship. Peter, in the midst of his despair, claimed it and returned with many tears. Judas chose death. Peter chose life. I realize that this choice is always before me. Constantly I am tempted to wallow in my own lostness and lose touch with my original goodness, my God-given humanity, my basic blessedness, and thus allow the powers of death to take charge. This happens over and over again whenever I say to myself: "I am no good. I am useless. I am worthless. I am unlovable. I am a nobody." There are always countless events and situations that I can single out to convince myself and others that my life is just not worth living, that I am only a burden, a problem, a source of conflict, or an exploiter of other people's time and energy. Many people live with this dark, inner sense of themselves. In contrast to the prodigal, they let the darkness absorb them so completely that there is no light left to turn toward and return to. They might not kill themselves physically, but spiritually they are no longer alive. They have given up faith in their original goodness and, thus, also in their Father who has given them their humanity.

But when God created man and woman in his own image, he saw that "it was very good," and, despite the dark voices, no man or woman can ever change that.

—*The Return of the Prodigal Son*

During this week Judas and Peter present me with the choice between running away from Jesus in despair or returning to him in hope. Judas betrayed Jesus and hanged himself. Peter denied Jesus and returned to him in tears.

Sometimes despair seems an attractive choice, solving everything in the negative. The voice of despair says, "I sin over and over again. After endless promises to myself and others to do better next time, I find myself back again in the old dark places. Forget about trying to change. I have tried for years. It didn't work and it will never work. It is better that I get out of people's way, be forgotten, no longer around, dead."

This strangely attractive voice takes all uncertainties away and puts an end to the struggle. It speaks unambiguously for the darkness and offers a clear-cut negative identity.

But Jesus came to open my ears to another voice that says, "I am your God, I have moulded you with my own hands, and I love what I have made. I love you with a love that has no limits, because I love you as I am loved. Do not run away from me. Come back to me—not once, not twice, but always again. You are my child. How can you ever doubt that I will embrace you again, hold you against my breast, kiss you, and let my hands run through your hair? I am your God—the God of mercy and compassion, the God of pardon and love, the God of tenderness and care. Please do not say that I have given up on you, that I cannot stand you anymore, that there is no way back. It is not true. I so much want you to be with me. I so much want you to be close to me. I know all your thoughts, I hear all your words. I see all of your actions. And I love you because you are beautiful, made in my own image, an expression of my most intimate love. Do not judge yourself. Do not condemn yourself. Do not reject yourself. Let my love touch the deepest, most hidden corners of your heart and reveal to you your own beauty, a beauty that you have lost sight of, but which will become visible to you again in the light of my mercy. Come, come, let me wipe your tears, and let my mouth come close to your ear and say to you, 'I love you, I love you, I love you.'"

This is always the voice that Jesus wants us to hear. It is the voice that calls us always to return to the one who has created us in love and wants to re-create us in mercy. Peter heard that voice and trusted it. As he let that voice touch his heart, tears came—tears of sorrow and tears of joy, tears of remorse and tears of peace, tears of repentance and tears of gratitude.

—*The Road to Daybreak*

MAUNDY THURSDAY

Just before entering on the road of his passion he washed the feet of his disciples and offered them his body and blood as food and drink. These two acts belong together. They are both an expression of God's determination to show us the fullness of his love. Therefore John introduces the story of the washing of the disciples' feet with the words: "Jesus . . . having loved those who were his in the world, loved them to the end" (John 13:1).

What is even more astonishing is that on both occasions Jesus commands us to do the same. After washing his disciples' feet, Jesus says, "I have given you an example so that you may copy what I have done to you" (John 13:15). After giving himself as food and drink, he says, "Do this in remembrance of me" (Luke 22:19). Jesus calls us to continue his mission of revealing the perfect love of God in this world. He calls us to total self-giving. He does not want us to keep anything for ourselves. Rather, he wants our love to be as full, as radical, and as complete as his own. He wants us to bend ourselves to the ground and touch the places in each other that most need washing. He also wants us to say to each other, "Eat of me and drink of me." By this complete nurturing, he wants us to become one body and one spirit, united by the love of God.

—*The Road to Daybreak*

In the Eucharist God's love is most concretely made present. Jesus has not only become human, he has also become bread and wine in order that, through our eating and our drinking, God's love might become our own. The great mystery of the Eucharist is that God's love is offered to us not in the abstract, but in a very concrete way; not as a theory, but as food for our daily life. The Eucharist opens the way for us to make God's love our own. Jesus himself makes that clear to us when he says:

> . . . my flesh is real food
> and my blood is real drink.
> Whoever eats my flesh and drinks my blood
> lives in me
> and I live in that person.
> As the living Father sent me
> and I draw life from the Father,
> so whoever eats me will also draw life from me.

Whenever you receive the body and blood of Jesus in the Eucharist, his love is given to you, the same love that he showed on the cross. It is the love of God for all people of all times and places, all religions and creeds, all races and classes, all tribes and nations, all sinners and saints.

—*Letters to Marc about Jesus*

"Can you drink the cup that I am going to drink?" Jesus asked his friends. They answered yes, but had no idea what he was talking about. Jesus' cup is the cup of sorrow, not just his own sorrow but the sorrow of the whole human race. It is a cup full of physical, mental, and spiritual anguish. It is the cup of starvation, torture, loneliness, rejection, abandonment, and immense anguish. It is the cup full of bitterness. Who wants to drink it? It is the cup that Isaiah calls "the cup of God's wrath. The chalice, the stupefying cup, you have drained to the dregs," (Isaiah 51:17) and what the second angel in the Book of Revelation calls "the wine of retribution" (Revelation 14:8), which Babylon gave the whole world to drink.

When the moment to drink that cup came for Jesus, he said: "My soul is sorrowful to the point of death" (Matthew 26:38). His agony was so intense that "his sweat fell to the ground like great drops of blood" (Luke 22:44). His close friends James and John, whom he had asked if they could drink the cup that he was going to drink, were there with him but fast asleep, unable to stay awake with him in his sorrow. In his immense loneliness, he fell on his face and cried out: "My Father, if it is possible, let this cup pass me by" (Matthew 26:39). Jesus couldn't face it. Too much pain to hold, too much suffering to embrace, too much agony to live through. He didn't feel he could drink that cup filled to the brim with sorrows.

Why then could he still say yes? I can't fully answer that question, except to say that beyond all the abandonment experienced in body and mind Jesus still had a spiritual bond with the one he called Abba. He possessed a trust beyond betrayal, a surrender beyond despair, a love beyond all fears. This intimacy beyond all human intimacies made it possible for Jesus to allow the request to let the cup pass him by become a prayer directed to the one who had called him "My Beloved." Notwithstanding his anguish, that bond of love had not been broken. It couldn't be felt in the body, nor thought through in the mind. But it was there, beyond all feelings and thoughts, and it maintained the communion underneath all disruptions. It was that spiritual sinew, that intimate communion with his Father, that made him hold on to the cup and pray: "My Father, let it be as you, not I, would have it" (Matthew 26:39).

Jesus didn't throw the cup away in despair. No, he kept it in his hands, willing to drink it to the dregs. This was not a show of willpower, staunch determination, or great heroism. This was a deep spiritual yes to Abba, the lover of his wounded heart.

—Can You Drink the Cup?

GOOD FRIDAY

Jesus stands before Pilate. He is silent. He does not defend himself against the many charges made against him. But when Pilate asks him, "What have you done?" he says, "I came into the world for this, to bear witness to the truth; and all who are on the side of truth listen to my voice" (John 18:35–8). The truth of which Jesus speaks is not a thesis, or a doctrine, or an intellectual explanation of reality. It is the very relationship, the life-giving intimacy between himself and the Father of which he wants us to partake. Pilate could not hear that, nor can anyone who is not connected to Jesus.

—Walk with Jesus

Pilate handed Jesus over to be scourged. The soldiers "stripped him and put a scarlet cloak around him, and having twisted thorns into a crown, they put this on his head and placed a reed in his right hand. To make fun of him they knelt to him saying: 'Hail, King of the Jews!' And they spat on him and took the reed and struck him on the head with it. And when they had finished making fun of him, they took off the cloak and dressed him in his own clothes and led him away to crucifixion" (Matthew 27:28–31). Jesus undergoes it all. The time of action is past. He does not speak any more; he does not protest; he does not reproach or admonish. He has become a victim. He no longer acts, but is acted upon. He has entered his passion.

—Walk with Jesus

When Jesus was carrying his cross to Golgotha, the soldiers came across a man from Cyrene, called Simon, and they enlisted him to carry the cross because it had become too heavy for Jesus alone.

He was unable to carry it to the place of his execution and needed the help of a stranger to fulfil his mission. So much weakness, so much vulnerability. Jesus needs to fulfil his mission. He needs people to carry the cross with him and for him. He came to us to show us the way to his Father's home. He came to offer us a new dwelling place, to give us a new sense of belonging, to point us to the true safety. But he cannot do it alone. The hard, painful work of salvation is a work in which God becomes dependent on human beings. Yes, God is full of power, glory, and majesty. But God chose to be among us as one of us—as a dependent human being.

—*Walk with Jesus*

Jesus was stripped. The soldiers threw dice to decide which of them would have his garment (see John 19:24). Nothing was left to him. He, the image of the unseen God, the first-born of all creation, in whom all things were created in heaven and on earth, everything visible and invisible, thrones, ruling forces, sovereignties, powers—he it was, being stripped of all power and dignity and exposed to the world in total vulnerability. Here the greatest mystery of all time was revealed to us: God chose to reveal the divine glory to us in humiliation. Where all beauty is gone, all eloquence silenced, all splendour taken away, and all admiration withdrawn, there it is that God has chosen to manifest unconditional love to us.

—*Walk with Jesus*

. . . One year, during Holy Week, a small group of theology students invited me to join them in a prayer vigil at Electric Boat, the nuclear submarine shipyard in Groton, Connecticut. . . . On Good Friday we went to Groton to witness for peace in front of the administration building of Electric Boat. The leaders of the group asked me to lead the community in the Stations of the Cross. . . . As a child I had often made these fourteen stations in church. They commemorate fourteen events between Jesus' being condemned to death by Pontius Pilate and his burial. These events have been vividly portrayed in paintings and sculpture, and I remember well how my Dutch teenage friends and I walked from station to station in the chapel of our high school, not once in a while, but many times a week during our lunch breaks.

But as I grew older, the Stations of the Cross soon became a pious childhood memory. The Second Vatican Council had so altered my religious consciousness that, along with most of my fellow Catholics, I dropped this devotional practice and focused on official liturgical celebration. Who would have dreamt that twenty years after the Council I would lead an ecumenical group of theology students in the Stations of the Cross on the streets of Gorton, Connecticut, in prayerful resistance against an impending nuclear holocaust?

We prayed fervently with words and songs as well as in silence. We heard the story of Jesus' suffering in a way that we could not have heard it in any church. It was hard for me to know fully how I felt, but something new was happening to me that I had never experienced before. It was the deep awareness that prayer was no longer a neutral event without danger. Moreover, the words I had so often spoken from pulpits about death and resurrection, about suffering and new life, suddenly received a new power, a power to unambiguously condemn death and call forth life.

   —*The Road to Peace*

Many people say, "I am not afraid of death, but I am afraid of dying." This is quite understandable, since dying often means illness, pain, dependency, and loneliness.

The fear of dying is nothing to be ashamed of. It is the most human of all human fears. Jesus himself entered into that fear. In his anguish "sweat fell to the ground like great drops of blood" (Luke 22:44). How must we deal with our fear of dying? Like Jesus we must pray that we may receive special strength to make the great passage to new life. Then we can trust that God will send us an angel to comfort us, as he sent an angel to Jesus.

   —*Bread for the Journey*

They all came, more than four hundred people—handicapped men and women and their assistants and friends. Everybody seemed to know very well what they were doing: expressing their love and gratitude for him who gave his life for them. As they were crowding around the cross and kissing the feet and the head of Jesus, I closed my eyes and could see his sacred body stretched out and crucified upon our planet earth. I saw the immense suffering of humanity during the centuries: people killing each other; people dying from starvation and epidemics; people driven from their homes; people sleeping on the streets of large cities; people clinging to each other in desperation; people flagellated, tortured, burned, and mutilated; people alone in locked flats, in prison dungeons, in labour camps; people craving a gentle word, a friendly letter, a consoling embrace, people—children, teenagers, adults, middle-aged, and elderly—all crying out with an anguished voice: "My God, my God, why have you forsaken us?"

Imagining the naked, lacerated body of Christ stretched out over our globe, I was filled with horror. But as I opened my eyes I saw Jacques, who bears the marks of suffering in his face, kiss the body with passion and tears in his eyes. I saw Ivan carried on Michael's back. I saw Edith coming in her wheelchair. As they came—walking or limping, seeing or blind, hearing or deaf—I saw the endless procession of humanity gathering around the sacred body of Jesus, covering it with their tears and their kisses, and slowly moving away from it comforted and consoled by such great love. There were signs of relief; there were smiles breaking through tear-filled eyes; there were hands in hands and arms in arms. With my mind's eye I saw the huge crowds of isolated, agonizing individuals walking away from the cross together, bound by the love they had seen with their own eyes and touched with their own lips. The cross of horror became the cross of hope, the tortured body became the body that gives new life; the gaping wounds became the source of forgiveness, healing, and reconciliation.

—*The Road to Daybreak*

About a hundred of us walked from the meeting hall to the Dayspring chapel, each carrying a stone to symbolize our burden and our brokenness. We stopped three times to remember how Jesus is condemned to death, Simon of Cyrene is forced to carry the cross when Jesus falls, and Veronica wipes Jesus' face with her towel. Jesus is nailed to the cross.

Michael, Adam's brother, dressed in an alb and with a crown of thorns on his head, is Jesus. An assistant helps him to carry the cross. At the third station there is an armchair for him to rest in. We sing and listen to reflections on the passion of Jesus. In the chapel we place our stones on or around the cross. Sitting together in chairs and on the floor we sing, "Behold, behold, the wood of the cross." Lorenzo hammers three big nails in the cross, piercing the silence. Then we sing again: "Were you there when they crucified my Lord? ... Were you there when they nailed him to the tree? ... Were you there when they laid him in the tomb? ... Sometimes it causes me to tremble, tremble, tremble."

Yes, it is a good Friday. In the midst of all the grief and mourning, there is sweet consolation. We are together, and there is love pouring out from our broken hearts and from the pierced heart of God.

—Sabbatical Journey

O dear Lord, what can I say to you on this holy night? Is there any word that could come from my mouth, any thought, any sentence? You died for me, you gave all for my sins, you not only became human for me but also suffered the most cruel death for me. Is there any response? I wish that I could find a fitting response, but in contemplating your Holy Passion and Death I can only confess humbly to you that the immensity of your divine love makes any response seem totally inadequate. Let me just stand and look at you. Your body is broken, your head wounded, your hands and feet are split open by nails, your side is pierced. Your dead body now rests in the arms of your Mother. It is all over now. It is finished. It is fulfilled. It is accomplished. Sweet Lord, gracious Lord, generous

Lord, forgiving Lord, I adore you, I praise you, I thank you. You have made all things new through your passion and death. Your cross has been planted in this world as the new sign of hope.

Let me always live under your cross, O Lord, and proclaim the hope of your cross unceasingly. Amen.

  —*A Cry for Mercy*

Jesus died. The powers of death crushed him. Not only the fear-ridden judgments of Pilate, the torture by the Roman soldiers, and the cruel crucifixion, but also the powers and principalities of this world. The world's death powers destroyed him. But the death of Jesus is the death of the Word "through whom all things came into being," and "what has come into being in him was life, life that was the light of people, and the light shines in the darkness, and darkness could not overpower it" (John 1:3–5).

Jesus was crushed by the powers of death, but his death removed death's sting. To those who believe in him he gave the power to become the children of God, that is, to participate in the life where death can no longer reach. By his death, Jesus was victorious over all the powers of death. The darkness in our hearts that makes us surrender to the power of death, the darkness in our society that makes us victims of violence, war, and destruction, has been dispelled by the light that shines forth from the One who gave his life as a complete gift to the God of life.

  —*Walk with Jesus*

Emptiness and fullness at first seem complete opposites. But in the spiritual life they are not. In the spiritual life we find the fulfilment of our deepest desires by becoming empty for God.

We must empty the cups of our lives completely to be able to receive the fullness of life from God. Jesus lived this on the cross. The moment of complete emptiness and complete fullness became the same. When he had given all away to his Abba, his dear Father, he cried out, "It is fulfilled" (John 19:30). He who was lifted up on the cross was also lifted into the resurrection. He who had emptied and humbled himself was raised up and "given the name above all other names" (see Philippians 2:7–9). Let us keep listening to Jesus' question: "Can you drink the cup that I am going to drink?" (Matthew 20:22)

—*Bread for the Journey*

To care for others requires an ever-increasing acceptance. This acceptance led Jesus and his disciples to where they did not want to go—to the cross. That is also the road of those who pray. When we are still young, you want to hold everything in your own hands, but when you have grown older and opened your hands in prayer, you are able to let yourself be led without knowing where. You know only that the freedom which God's breath has brought you will lead to new life, even if the cross is the only sign you can see.

—*With Open Hands*

HOLY SATURDAY

On the seventh day of the week of our redemption, when Jesus had fulfilled all he was sent by his Father to do, he rested in the tomb, and the women whose hearts were broken with grief rested with him. Of all the days in history, Holy Saturday—the Saturday during which the body of Jesus lay in the tomb in silence and darkness behind the large stone that was rolled against its entrance (Mark 15:46)—is the day of God's solitude. It is the day on which the whole creation waits in deep inner rest. It is the day on which no words are spoken, no proclamations made. The Word of God through whom all had been made lay buried in the darkness of the earth. This Holy Saturday is the most quiet of all days. Its quiet connects the first covenant with the second, the people of Israel with the not-yet-knowing world, the Temple with the new worship in the Spirit, the sacrifices of blood with the sacrifice of bread and wine, the Law with the Gospel. This divine silence is the most fruitful silence that the world has ever known. From this silence, the Word will be spoken again and make all things new.

—*Walk with Jesus*

Easter

Season of Hope

Easter

The Easter mystery of Christ's death and resurrection lies at the heart of the Church's liturgical life. In the spirit of the Risen Jesus, we are urged during the next fifty days to journey, as one liturgical prayer book puts it, "on a high plateau." The way is "smooth and peaceful, full of joy in the certitude that the Lord is living." It is a season of joyous thanksgiving. After the ceremonies of Holy Week, it can sometimes seem like an anti-climax. But Easter should be proclaimed as a time for celebration and companionship on the Emmaus Road, an opportunity for dispelling doubt and bringing reassurance to all we meet along the way.

Henri Nouwen was realistic about this season of hope. He acknowledged that there can still be a painful awareness of sinfulness as well as fear but there is also light breaking through. Something new is happening. Something that goes beyond the changing moods of our life. The stream of God's presence runs beneath our undulating waves of temperament. Nouwen felt that Easter brings the awareness that God is active even when his presence is not directly noticed.

Whatever the headlines, Easter announces the news that evil has ultimately been overcome by good.

This season embraces Ascensiontide when the Church commemorates the return of Jesus to heaven. It is a feast centred round a separation sustained by a blessing. At this time of year I always think of the late leader

119

of the British Labour Party, John Smith. He died suddenly on Ascension
Day. I remember praying for him publicly that evening during a service for
Ascension broadcast on BBC Radio 4. He was buried on Iona, an island of
wild beauty off the west coast of Scotland held by tradition to be "near-
est to heaven." In a later interview, Elizabeth Smith told me how she and
her husband had fallen in love with Iona and spent their holidays there. It
was one of the few places where the politician could unwind and relax
almost instantaneously. It had been a particular honour for him to be
buried there because the graveyard was usually reserved for islanders.

Like many bereaved families (and the disciples themselves), the Smiths
went through a period of great shock, numbness, and incomprehension
after John's death. But Elizabeth revealed that at the time she felt "an
incredible feeling of peace and calm" which she had not expected. It had
given her great strength to cope with the sense of loss and separation.

Easter is about acknowledging the breaking in of eternity into the ordinary patterns of our lives. In this selection of writings, we share Henri
Nouwen's undisguised joy in the resurrection, symbolised so resplendent-
ly by the sun in the paintings of van Gogh.

Easter is a bodily experience, celebrating in every fiber new life, new
hope, and ecstatic liberation.

EASTER DAY

Dear Lord, risen Lord, light of the world, to you be all praise and
glory! This day, so full of your presence, your joy, your peace, is
indeed your day.

I just returned from a walk through the dark woods. It was cool
and windy, but everything spoke of you. Everything: the clouds,
the trees, the wet grass, the valley with its distant lights, the sound
of the wind. They all spoke of your resurrection; they all made me
aware that everything is indeed good. In you all is created good,
and by you all creation is renewed and brought to an even greater
glory than it possessed at its beginning.

As I walked through the dark woods at the end of this day, full of
intimate joy, I heard you call Mary Magdalene by her name and

heard how you called from the shore of the lake to your friends to throw out their nets. I also saw you entering the closed room where your disciples were gathered in fear. I saw you appearing on the mountain and at the outskirts of the village. How intimate these events really are. They are like special favours to dear friends. They were not done to impress or overwhelm anyone, but simply to show that your love is stronger than death.

O Lord, I know now that it is in silence, in a quiet moment, in a forgotten corner that you will meet me, call me by name and speak to me a word of peace. It is in my stillest hour that you became the risen Lord to me.

Dear Lord, I am so grateful for all you have given me this past week. Stay with me in the days to come. Bless all who suffer in this world and bring peace to your people, whom you loved so much that you gave your life for them. Amen.

—*A Cry for Mercy*

PEOPLE OF THE RESURRECTION

After the Gospel reading I reflected on the significance of our faith in the resurrection of the body. As a community of people conscious of our disabilities, we are held together not so much by the Word as by the body. Although we may use many words and there is a lot of "talk" among us, it is the weak bodies of our core members that create community. We wash, shave, comb, dress, clean, feed, and hold the bodies of those who are entrusted to us and thus build a communal body. As we claim our faith in the resurrection of the body, we come to see that the resurrection is not simply an event after death but a reality of everyday life. Our care for the body calls us to unity beyond organization, to intimacy beyond eroticism, and to integrity beyond psychological wholeness.

Unity, intimacy, and integrity are the three spiritual qualities of the resurrected life. We are called to break through the boundaries of nationality, race, sexual orientation, age, and mental capacities and create a unity of love that allows the weakest among us to live well. We are called to go far beyond the place of lust, sexual need, and desire for physical union to a spiritual intimacy that involves body, mind, and heart. And we are called to let go of old ways of feeling good about ourselves and reach out to a new integration of the many facets of our humanity. These calls are calls to the resurrection while anticipating it in our daily lives through spiritual unity, intimacy, and integrity.

As I talked about these things it seemed that those who were present at the vigil could recognize some of what I spoke about in their daily Daybreak life.

As we received the Body and Blood of Jesus, I was struck by the *real* quality of the paschal mystery. We are the people of the resurrection, living our lives with a great vision that transforms us as we are living it.

—*Sabbatical Journey*

INTIMATE ENCOUNTERS

It was not a spectacular event forcing people to believe. Rather, it was an event for the friends of Jesus, for those who had known him, listened to him, and believed in him. It was a very intimate event: a word here, a gesture there, and a gradual awareness that something new was being born—small, hardly noticed, but with the potential to change the face of the earth. Mary of Magdala heard her name. John and Peter saw the empty grave. Jesus' friends felt their hearts burn in encounters that find expression in the remarkable words "He is risen." All had remained the same, while all had changed.

—*The Road to Daybreak*

SPIRITUAL EMPOWERMENT

Today I was thinking how nobody recognizes Jesus immediately. They think he is the gardener, a stranger, or a ghost. But when a familiar gesture is there again—breaking bread, inviting the disciples to try for another catch, calling them by name—his friends know he is there for them. Absence and presence are touching each other. The old Jesus is gone. They no longer can be with him as before. The new Jesus, the risen Lord, is there, intimately, more intimately than ever. It is an empowering presence. "Do not cling to me . . . but go . . . and tell" (John 20:17).

The resurrection stories reveal the always-present tension between coming and leaving, intimacy and distance, holding and letting go, at-homeness and mission, presence and absence. We face that tension every day. It puts us on the journey to the full realization of the promise given to us. "Do not cling to me" might mean "This is not heaven yet" but also "I am now within you and empower you for a spiritual task in the world, continuing what I have begun. You are the living Christ."

While many question whether the resurrection really took place, I wonder if it doesn't take place every day if we have the eyes to see and the ears to hear.

—*Sabbatical Journey*

A SIGN OF LOVE

The resurrection of Jesus was a hidden event. Jesus didn't rise from the grave to baffle his opponents, to make a victory statement, or to prove to those who crucified him that he was right after all. Jesus rose as a sign to those who loved him and followed him that God's divine love is stronger than death. To the women and men who committed themselves to him, he revealed that his mission had been fulfilled. To those who shared in his ministry, he gave the sacred task to call all people into the new life within him.

The world didn't take notice. Only those whom he called by name, with whom he broke bread and to whom he spoke words of peace, were aware of what happened. Still, it was this hidden event that freed humanity from the shackles of death.

—Bread for the Journey

NEW LIFE

When Jesus appeared to his disciples after his resurrection, he convinced them that he was not a ghost but the same one that they had known as their teacher and friend. To his frightened and doubtful friends he said: "See by my hands and my feet that it is I myself. Touch me and see for yourselves" (Luke 24:39). Then he asked them for something to eat, and later, when he appeared to them for the third time, he offered them breakfast, bread, and fish (see Luke 24:42–3 and John 21:12–14).

But Jesus also showed them that his body was a new spiritual body, no longer subject to the laws of nature. While the doors of the room where the disciples had gathered were closed, Jesus came and stood among them (see John 20:19), and when he offered them breakfast, nobody dared to ask: "Who are you?" They knew it was Jesus, their Lord and teacher, but they also knew that he no longer belonged to their world (see John 21:12). It was this experience of the risen Jesus that revealed to his disciples the life in the resurrection that was awaiting them. Are there any experiences in our lives that give us a hint of the new life that has been promised us?

—Bread for the Journey

THE MYSTERY OF ART
A Reflection on Rembrandt's The Pilgrims of Emmaus

Jesus sits behind the table looking up in prayer while holding a loaf of bread in his hands. On his right, one of the pilgrims leans backwards with his hands folded; while on his left, the other has moved his chair away from the table and gazes with utter attention at Jesus. Behind him a humble servant, obviously unaware of what is happening, reaches forward to put a plate of food on the table. On the table, a bright white cloth only partially covers the heavy table rug. There are very few objects on the table: three pewter plates, a knife, and two small cups. Jesus sits in front of a majestic stone apse flanked by two big, square pillars. On the right side of the painting, the entrance door is visible, and there is a coat stand in the corner over which a cape has been casually thrown. In the left corner of the room, a doglike figure can be seen lying under a bench. The whole painting is in endless varieties of brown: light brown, dark brown, yellow-brown, red-brown, and so on. The source of light is not revealed, but the white tablecloth is the brightest part of the painting. . . .

As we looked at the painting [in the Louvre, Paris], many people passed by. One of the guides said, "Look at Jesus' face, in ecstasy, yet so humble." That expressed beautifully what we saw. Jesus' face is full of light, a light which radiates from his head in a cloudlike halo. He does not look at the men around him. His eyes look upward in an expression of intimate communion with the Father. While Jesus is in deep prayer, he yet remains present; he remains the humble servant who came to be among us and show us the way to God.

The longer we looked at the painting, the more we felt drawn into the mystery it expresses . . . As we continued to let the painting speak to us, we were amazed that we both came to see it more and more as a call to worship Christ in the Eucharist. The hands of Jesus holding the bread on the white altar table cloth are the center not only of the light, but also of the sacramental action. Yet if Jesus were to leave the altar, the bread would still be there. And we would still be able to be with him.

For an instant the museum became a church, the painting a sanctuary, and Rembrandt a priest. All of it told me something about God's hidden presence in the world.

 —*The Road to Daybreak*

VAN GOGH'S MOUNTAIN

Dear Lord, after your resurrection you opened the minds of your disciples to understand the Scriptures. You made it clear to them that Moses, the prophets, and the psalmist had spoken about you. You revealed to them the great mystery that it was ordained that you should suffer and so enter into your glory.

Tonight I pray to you for an always deeper understanding of the Scriptures and an always greater awareness that you are in the center, or—to say it with the words of Vincent van Gogh—that your Gospel is the top of the mountain of which the Old Testament and the letters of the Apostles are the slopes. Let me see your presence in the psalms, in the prophets, and in the great story of the people of Israel, and let this insight help me better understand my own history, my own struggle, and my own pain.

Please, Lord, join me on the road, enter into my closed room, and take my foolishness away. Open my mind and heart to the great mystery of your active presence in my life, and give me the courage to help others discover your presence in their lives.

Thank you, Lord, for this day. Amen.

—*A Cry for Mercy*

VAN GOGH'S SUN

Dear Lord, free me from my dark past, into which I often feel myself falling as if into a deep cistern. You are the light that has come into the world so that whoever believes in you need not stay in darkness any longer. Do not allow me to sink back into my own dark pit, O Lord, but let your warm, gentle, life-giving light lift me from my grave. Vincent van Gogh painted you as the sun when he painted the resurrection of Lazarus. In so doing, he wanted to express his own liberation from a dark, imprisoning past. Lord, keep showing me your light, and give me the strength to rise and follow you without ever looking back. You are my Strength, my

Refuge, and my Stronghold. As long as I keep my eyes on you, there is no reason to return to past events, past patterns, past ideas. In your light all becomes new. Let me be fully yours. Amen.

—A Cry for Mercy

LIVING IN ECSTASY

Jesus connects joy with the promise of seeing him again. In this sense, it is similar to the joy we experience when a dear friend returns after a long absence. But Jesus makes it clear that joy is more than that. It is "his own joy," flowing from the love he shares with his heavenly Father and leading to completion. "Remain in my love . . . so that my joy may be in you and your joy may be complete" (John 15:9b, and 11).

The word "ecstasy" helps us to understand more fully the joy that Jesus offers. The literal meaning of the word can help to guide our thinking about joy. "Ecstasy" comes from the Greek "ekstasis," which in turn is derived from "ek." meaning out, and "stasis," a state of standstill. To be ecstatic literally means to be outside of a static place. Thus, those who live ecstatic lives are always moving away from rigidly fixed situations and exploring new, unmapped dimensions of reality. Here we see the essence of joy. Joy is always new. Whereas there can be old pain, old grief, and old sorrow, there can be no old joy. Old joy is not joy! Joy is always connected with movement, renewal, rebirth, change—in short, with life.

Joy is essentially ecstatic since it moves out of the place of death, which is rigid and fixed, and into the place of life which is new and surprising. "God is God not of the dead but of the living" (Matthew 22:32). There is no tinge of death in God. God is pure life. Therefore, living in the house of God is living in a state of constant ecstasy, in which we always experience the joy of being alive.

—In the House of the Lord

HUMMING IN THE DARKNESS

Hope means to keep living
amid desperation
and to keep humming
in the darkness.
Hoping is knowing that there is love,
it is trust in tomorrow
it is falling asleep
and waking again
when the sun rises.
In the midst of a gale at sea,
it is to discover land.
In the eyes of another
it is to see that you are understood. . . .

As long as there is still hope
There will also be prayer. . . .

And you will be held
in God's hands.

   —With Open Hands

Feasts of Easter

THE ASCENSION

Dear Lord, at the end of this Ascension Day I am filled with gratitude. I realize that on this day you concluded your stay among us and the great mystery of your incarnation became visible in its fullness. Your earthly life, which began with Gabriel's visit to your Mother, was concluded when you were lifted up in a cloud and taken from the sight of your disciples. You, O Lord, Son of God, Son of Man, Emmanuel, Messiah, Redeemer of all people, you indeed shared with us all that is human and led our humanity to the right hand of your Heavenly Father. When you were no longer seen by your friends and had left them behind, you had fulfilled your divine mission. You taught us all we need to know; you did all that could be done; you gave us all that you had.

What would my life have been without knowing you? All my joys and pains are connected with your having come into this world.

Thank you, Lord, for your life on this earth and for calling me to tell the story of your life to all people. Amen.

—*A Cry for Mercy*

GEORGE, Martyr, Patron of England, c. 304
(23 April)

Good shepherds are willing to lay down their lives for their sheep
(see John 10:11). As spiritual leaders walking in the footsteps of
Jesus, we are called to lay down our lives for our people. This laying down might in special circumstances mean dying for others.
But it means first of all making our own lives—our sorrows and
joys, our despair and hope, our loneliness and experience of intimacy—available to others as sources of new life.

—*Bread for the Journey*

MARK THE EVANGELIST
(25 April)

The contemplative life is a life in which time slowly loses its
opaqueness and becomes transparent. This is often a very difficult
and slow process, but it is full of re-creating power. To start seeing
that the many events of our day, week, or year are not in the way
of our search for a full life, but rather the way to it, is a real experience of conversion. If we start discovering that writing letters,
attending classes, visiting people, and cooking food are not a series
of random events that prevent us from realizing our deepest self,
but contain within themselves the transforming power we are looking for, then we are beginning to move from time lived as *chronos* to
time lived as *kairos*. *Kairos* means *the* opportunity. It is the right time,
the real moment, the chance of our life. When our time becomes
kairos, it opens up endless new possibilities and offers us a constant
opportunity for a change of heart.

In Jesus' life every event becomes *kairos*. He opens his public
ministry with the words, "The time has come" (Mark 1:15), and he
lives every moment of it as an opportunity. Finally, he announces
that his time is near and enters into his last hours as *the kairos*. In so
doing he liberates history from fatalistic chronology.

This really is good news because now we know that all the events
of life, even such dark events as war, famine and flood, violence

and murder, are not irreversible fatalities but rather carry within themselves the possibility of becoming the moment of change.

—*Clowning in Rome*

PHILIP AND JAMES, APOSTLES
(1 or 3 May)

Dear Lord, your apostle Philip joined an Ethiopian pilgrim returning from Jerusalem to his country. As you did when you joined the men going to Emmaus, so your apostle explained the Scriptures to this pilgrim and made it clear that they were speaking about you. I pray that this will be my ministry: to join people on their journey and to open their eyes to see you. Many people are searching. Often they are studying, reading, discussing, writing, and performing to find an answer to their most intimate questions. But many remain groping in the dark. Give me the courage to join them and say to them as Philip did, "Did you understand what you were reading?" Give me the intelligence and conviction to speak to them about you, who are the Way, the Truth, and the Life. Give me the discernment to know when they are ready to be baptized by water and the Holy Spirit.

But, please, Lord, also give me the encouragement you gave to Philip when you said to him, "Go up and meet that chariot." You know that I am shy and fearful. Let me be confident and free. Amen.

—*A Cry for Mercy*

Probably no New Testament writer is as explicit about the importance of concrete acts of service as James. He writes, "Pure, unspoilt religion, in the eyes of God our Father is this: coming to the help of orphans and widows when they need it, and keeping oneself uncontaminated by the world" (James 1:27). With considerable irony, James shows to the "twelve tribes of the Dispersion" —i.e., the Jewish Christians scattered all over the Graeco-Roman world—the importance of concrete acts of service.

—*Compassion*

MATTHIAS THE APOSTLE
(14 May)

Each of us has a mission in life. Jesus prays to his Father for his followers, saying: "As you sent me into the world, I have sent them into the world" (John 17:18).

We seldom realise fully that we are sent to fulfill God-given tasks. We act as if we have to choose how, where, and with whom to live. We act as if we were simply dropped down in creation and have to decide how to entertain ourselves until we die. But we were sent into the world by God, just as Jesus was. Once we start living our lives with that conviction, we will soon know what we were sent to do.

—Bread for the Journey

THE VISIT OF THE BLESSED VIRGIN MARY
TO ELIZABETH
(31 May)

Two women [Mary and Elizabeth] who felt oppressed and isolated suddenly realize their greatness and are free to celebrate their blessing. The two of them become community. They need each other, just to be together and protect each other, support each other, and affirm each other. They stay together for three months. Then each of them is ready to face her truth without fear, willing to suffer the consequences of her motherhood.

I can hardly think of a better way to understand friendship, care, and love than "the way of the visitation." In a world so full of shame and guilt, we need to visit each other and offer each other a safe place where we can claim our freedom and celebrate our gifts. We need to get away once in a while from the suspicious voices and angry looks and be in a place where we are deeply understood and loved. Then we might be able to face the hostile world again, without fear and with new trust in our integrity.

—Sabbatical Journey

I am deeply moved by this simple and mysterious encounter. In the midst of an unbelieving, doubting, pragmatic, and cynical world, two women meet each other and affirm in each other the promise given to them. The humanly impossible has happened to them. God has come to them to begin the salvation promised through the ages. Through these two women God has decided to change the course of history. Who could ever understand? Who could ever believe it? Who could ever let it happen? But Mary says, "Let it happen to me," and she immediately realizes that only Elizabeth will be able to affirm her "yes." For three months Mary and Elizabeth live together and encourage each other to truly accept the motherhood given to them. Mary's presence makes Elizabeth more fully aware of becoming the mother of the "prophet of the Most High" (Luke 1:76), and Elizabeth's presence allows Mary to grow in the knowledge of becoming the mother of the "Son of the Most High" (Luke 1:32).

Neither Mary nor Elizabeth had to wait in isolation. They could wait together and thus deepen in each other their faith in God, for whom nothing is impossible. Thus, God's most radical intervention into history was listened to and received in community.

The story of the Visitation teaches me the meaning of friendship and community. How can I ever let God's grace fully work in my life unless I live in a community of people who can affirm it, deepen it, and strengthen it? We cannot live this new life alone. God does not want to isolate us by his grace. On the contrary, he wants us to form new friendships and a new community—holy places where his grace can grow to fullness and bear fruit.

—*The Road to Daybreak*

Pentecost

Season of the Spirit

Pentecost

Pentecost is a dramatic moment in the liturgical year when the Spirit of God, "aflame with his fire." fills the universe and tells of a new heaven and a new earth. Fifty days after Easter, the Spirit showers down on the apostles, signifying the birth of the Church and salvation for all in Jesus Christ. Whit Sunday inaugurates a season of joy, hope, and mission, a time when the Church comes "alive with a new breath."

These quotations written by a Benedictine monk give a sense of the energy and passion released at Pentecost, signifying not only an historical event or a revealed truth but a spiritual reality. The red tongues of fire sometimes depicted by artists and iconographers are reminiscent of van Gogh's evergreen cypresses, which grow upwards "like green flaming tongues" as one commentator describes them. Their unbridled growth and untamed energy unleash a natural force of cosmic potential.

Pentecost is the season of spiritual energy and political dynamism.

Henri Nouwen believed that if people lived the spiritual life radically, it would affect everything they touched. Not only would it have an impact on personal growth and relationships, it would also influence economics, politics, and social structures. But, none the less, one didn't live the spiritual life with the deliberate intention to make political changes or induce social transformation.

"The people who have most influence in politics are often those who are least directly focusing on it," he told me, citing the witness of St Benedict, whose feast day falls at this time. "Benedict changed the whole European culture not by trying to be a politician but by trying to be faithful to God and to his community. The Benedictines had an enormous effect on the social and political structures of Europe but not because they were interested in changing political structures. They were interested in being obedient to God, not being politically relevant. A lot of great saints and great spiritual people have had enormous political effect but not because they were after the effect themselves."

I saw something of this same spirit of humility and influence in the late Cardinal Basil Hume, a Benedictine monk of Ampleforth who became leader of the Roman Catholic Church in England and Wales. Sometimes the Spirit impelled him to intervene on political issues: "When good and evil are at stake, or when it's a question of what is good for these particular human beings, then they become moral questions," he once told me. "I think there is a way of trying to win other people to your point of view in a manner which respects the other person and recognises that the other person is probably carrying great burdens as well."

Pentecost is the season when we are called to witness to the ends of the earth, no matter the political, cultural, or religious obstacles that might compromise our spiritual integrity. We might even be impelled to speak out in the name of truth and justice, knowing that derision or isolation might be our only rewards. In the following selections, Henri Nouwen invites us into the inner life of God and encourages us to claim the Spirit as the guiding light of our lives, burning away our fears and anxieties and setting us free to move wherever we are sent.

THE RE-CREATING POWER OF LOVE

. . . Pentecost is the coming of the Spirit of Jesus into the world. It is the celebration of God breaking through the boundaries of time and space and opening the whole world for the re-creating power of love. Pentecost is freedom, the freedom of the Spirit to blow where it wants.

Without Pentecost the Christ-event—the life, death, and resurrection of Jesus—remains imprisoned in history as something to remember, think about, and reflect on. The Spirit of Jesus comes to dwell within us, so that we can become living Christs here and now. Pentecost lifts the whole mystery of salvation out of its particularities and makes it into something universal, embracing all peoples, all countries, all seasons, and all eras. Pentecost is also the moment of empowering. Each individual human being can claim the Spirit of Jesus as the guiding spirit of his or her life. In that Spirit we can speak and act freely and confidently with the knowledge that the same Spirit that inspired Jesus is inspiring us.

—*Sabbatical Journey*

THE BREATH OF LIFE

When we speak about the Holy Spirit, we speak about the breath of God, breathing in us. The Greek word for "spirit" is *pneuma*, which means "breath." We are seldom aware of our breathing. It is so essential for life that we only think about it when something is wrong with it.

The Spirit of God is like our breath. God's spirit is more intimate to us than we are to ourselves. We might not often be aware of it, but without it we cannot live a "spiritual life." It is the Holy Spirit of God who prays in us, who offers us the gifts of love, forgiveness, kindness, goodness, gentleness, peace, and joy. It is the Holy Spirit who offers us the life that death cannot destroy. Let us always pray: "Come, Holy Spirit, come."

—*Bread for the Jour*

RENEWING THE WORLD

Dear Lord, when your Spirit descended upon your disciples, they spoke the languages of those who came to hear their witness. Tonight I pray that in our time your Spirit will also break through the many barriers that divide nations and people. Let there be unity among us who inhabit this world. Give us the strength to transcend our physical, emotional, and psychological differences and recognize that it is your Holy Spirit who unites us by making us all participants in your own divine life. Let your Spirit open our eyes and ears to your ongoing presence among us. Let us recognize you when we serve each other, work together for reconciliation and peace, and unite our talents to build a better world. Without your Spirit we are powerless, but with and in your Spirit we can renew the world. Do not leave us alone, but let your Spirit enter into our hearts so that together we can prepare the day of your glorious return, and can praise you, thank you, honour you, and love you all the days of our lives. Amen.

—*A Cry for Mercy*

THE INNER LIFE OF GOD

"The Descent of the Holy Spirit," a Russian icon painted toward the end of the 15th century, has reminded me forcefully that a life in the Spirit is in essence a life in community. Although I have always known this intellectually, a long and deep encounter with this Pentecost icon from the Russian Novgorod School has gradually allowed this knowledge of the head to become a knowledge of the heart.

That God reveals the fullness of divine love first of all in community, and that the proclamation of the good news finds its main source there has radical consequences for our lives. Because now the question is no longer: How can I best develop my spiritual life and share it with others? but Where do we find the community of faith to which the Spirit of God descends and from which God's message of hope and love can be brought as a light into the world? Once this question becomes our main concern we can no longer separate the spiritual life from life in community, belonging to God from belonging to each other and seeing Christ from seeing one another in him.

As I spent more time with this Pentecost icon, I gradually saw many new aspects of the spiritual life that other icons had not revealed to me. First, I saw how God is revealed to us at Pentecost as the God within. Then I perceived how this God within creates a new community of faith in which unity and diversity deepen each other. Finally, I discovered how this community of faith forms a vital center from which the liberation of the world can proceed.

. . . Pentecost completes the mystery of God's revelation as Father, Son, and Holy Spirit, and invites us to become fully part of the inner life of God. By becoming not only a God-for-us and a God-with-us, but also a God-within-us, God offers us the full knowledge of the divine life according to the promise of Jesus:

> "The Holy Spirit,
> whom the Father will send in my name,
> will teach you everything."
>
> —(*John 14:26*)

The Pentecost icon draws us into the heart of the mystery of God's self-revelation. The way the apostles and evangelists are gathered together manifests the presence of the God-within. The open space portrayed between the central figures of Peter and Paul, as well as the open space created by the half oval in which the twelve are seated, indicate the new, inner space where the Spirit dwells. Jesus is no longer with his disciples. He is risen. But his absence is not an emptiness. On the contrary, his departure has created the space in which his followers can receive the fullness of the Spirit. Jesus himself had prepared them by saying,

> "It is for your own good that I am going,
> because unless I go
> the Paraclete [the Spirit] will not come to you;
> but if I do go,
> I will send him to you. . . .
> He will lead you to the complete truth."
>
> —(*John 16:7, 13*)

With these words Jesus points forward to the new life in the Spirit that will be revealed at Pentecost. It will be a life lived in "complete truth." Closely related to the word "betrothal," the "complete truth" means full intimacy with God, a betrothal in which the complete divine life is given to us.

—*Behold the Beauty of the Lord*

GIVING AND RECEIVING

The fruits of the Spirit of God—joy, peace, patience, kindness, goodness, trustfulness, gentleness, and self-control (Galatians 5:22–3)—cannot be limited to interpersonal relationships. They have dimensions which far exceed the small circles of friends, family, and community. They carry in themselves a worldwide dynamic that we call mission. . . .

One of the most compelling qualities of life in the Spirit of Jesus is that we are always being sent out to bring and receive the gifts of God to and from all peoples and nations. It is spiritually impossible to enter into the house of God and to meet there all of humanity without coming to the inner awareness that the fruits of the Spirit grow and mature in a worldwide process of giving and receiving.

—*In the House of the Lord*

Feasts of Pentecost

FEAST OF THE HOLY TRINITY
(First Sunday after Pentecost)

About twenty people sat in a large circle in the lovely fenced-in garden. I tried to explain the mystery of the Trinity by saying that all human relationships are reflections of the relationships within God. God is the Lover, the Beloved, and the Love that binds us in unity. God invites us to be part of that inner movement of love so that we can truly become sons and daughters of the Father, sisters and brothers of the Son, and spouses of the Holy Spirit. Thus, all our human relationships can be lived in God, and as witness to God's divine presence in our lives.

I am deeply convinced that most human suffering comes from broken relationships. Anger, jealousy, resentment, and feelings of rejection all find their source in conflict between people who yearn for unity, community, and a deep sense of belonging. By claiming the Holy Trinity as home for our relational lives, we claim the truth that God gives us what we most desire and offers us the grace to forgive each other for not being perfect in love.

—*Sabbatical Journey*

To live in the world without belonging to the world summarizes the essence of the spiritual life. The spiritual life keeps us aware that our true house is not the house of fear, in which the powers of hatred and violence rule, but the house of love, where God resides.

Hardly a day passes in our lives without our experience of inner and outer fears, anxieties, apprehensions and preoccupations. These dark powers have pervaded every part of our world to such a degree that we can never fully escape them. Still it is possible not to belong to these powers, not to build our dwelling place among them, but to choose the house of love as our home. This choice is made not just once and for all but by living a spiritual life, praying at all times, and thus breathing God's breath. Through the spiritual life we gradually move from the house of fear to the house of love.

I have never seen the house of love more beautifully expressed than in the icon of the Holy Trinity, painted by Andrew Rublev in 1425 in memory of the great Russian saint, Sergius (1313–92). For me the contemplation of this icon has increasingly become a way to enter more deeply into the mystery of divine life while remaining fully engaged in the struggles of our hate-and-fear-filled world.

Andrew Rublev painted this icon not only to share the fruits of his own meditation on the mystery of the Holy Trinity but also to offer his fellow monks a way to keep their hearts centered in God while living in the midst of political unrest. The more we look at this holy image with the eyes of faith, the more we come to realize that it is painted not as a lovely decoration for a convent church, nor as a helpful explanation of a difficult doctrine, but as a holy place to enter and stay within. As we place ourselves in front of the icon in prayer, we come to experience a gentle invitation to participate in the intimate conversation that is taking place among the three divine angels and to join them around the table. The movement from the Father toward the Son and the movement of both Son and Spirit toward the Father become a movement in which the one who prays is lifted up and held secure.

—*Behold the Beauty of the Lord*

CORPUS CHRISTI
(Thursday after Trinity Sunday)

The Lord is the center of all things and yet in such a quiet, un-obtrusive, elusive way. He lives with us, even physically, but not in the same physical way that other elements are present to us. The transcendent physical presence is what characterizes the Eucharist. It is already the other world present in this one. In the celebration of the Eucharist we are given an enclave in our world of space and time. God in Christ is really here, and yet his physical presence is not characterized by the same limitations of space and time that we know.

The Eucharist can be seen only by those who already love the Lord and believe in his active, loving presence to us. But is that not true of every good relationship that we have? Friendship is like that, human love is like that. The bonds that unite us with those we love are invisible bonds. They become visible only indirectly, only by what we do as a result of them. But the bonds themselves are invisible. The presence of friends to one another is very real; this presence is palpably physical, sustaining us in difficult or joyful moments, and yet invisible.

—*The Genesee Diary*

The greatest mystery of the Christian faith is that God came to us in the body, suffered with us in the body, rose in the body, and gave us his body as food. No religion takes the body as seriously as the Christian religion. The body is not seen as the enemy or as a prison of the spirit, but celebrated as the spirit's temple. Through Jesus' birth, life, death, and resurrection, the human body has become part of the life of God. By eating the body of Christ, our own fragile bodies are becoming intimately connected with the risen Christ and thus prepared to be lifted up with him into the divine life. Jesus says, "I am the living bread which has come down from heaven. Anyone who eats this bread will live forever; and the bread that I shall give is my flesh, for the life of the world" (John 6:51).

It is in union with the body of Christ that I come to know the full significance of my own body. My own body is much more than a mortal instrument of pleasure and pain. It is a home where God wants to manifest the fullness of the divine glory. This truth is the most profound basis for the moral life. The abuse of the body—whether it be psychological (e.g., instilling fear), physical (e.g., torture), economic (e.g., exploitation), or sexual (e.g., hedonistic pleasure seeking)—is a distortion of true human destiny: to live in the body eternally with God. The loving care given to our bodies and the bodies of others is therefore a truly spiritual act, since it leads the body closer toward its glorious existence.

. . . The feast of the body of Christ is given to us to fully recognize the mystery of the body and to help us find ways to live reverently and joyfully in the body in expectation of the risen life with God.

—The Road to Daybreak

Spiritual life is life lived in the spirit of Jesus. I've spoken of the Eucharist as being the center of that life. Jesus is more, much more, than an important historical figure who can still inspire us today. In the Eucharist, he sets us free from constraint and compulsion, unites our suffering with his, forms a fellowship in shared vulnerability, offers us a love that forgives even our enemies and helps us to see God in the seclusion of the human heart. Where the Eucharist is, there Jesus really is present; there too the Church really is a body, and there we really do share, even now, in eternal life.

—Letters to Marc about Jesus

SACRED HEART OF JESUS
(Friday following Second Sunday after Pentecost)

Dear Lord Jesus. . . .

Your heart is not a heart of stone but a heart of flesh; your heart of flesh is not narrowed by human sin and unfaithfulness, but is as wide and deep as divine love itself. Your heart does not distinguish between rich and poor, friend and enemy, female and male, slave and free, sinner and saint. Your heart is open to receive anyone with total, unrestricted love. For anyone who wants to come to you, there is room. You want to draw all people to yourself and offer them a home where every human desire is met, every human longing comes to rest, and every human need is satisfied.

But your heart is gentle and humble. You do not force; you do not pull or push; you do not coerce. You want us to come freely to your heart and trust that we will find there the peace and joy we most desire. You do not put any requirement on us; you do not expect any great act of generosity; you do not hope for heroic gestures or dramatic signs. The only thing you want is trust. You can only give your heart to those who come to it in trust.

> —*Heart Speaks to Heart*

Dear Lord Jesus. . . .

Your broken heart is the source of my salvation, the foundation of my hope, the cause of my love. It is the sacred place where all that was, is, and ever shall be is held in unity. There all suffering has been suffered, all anguish lived, all loneliness endured, all abandonment felt and all agony cried out. There, human and divine love have kissed, and there God and all men and women of history are reconciled. All the tears of the human race have been cried there, all pain understood, and all despair touched. Together with all people of all times, I look up to you whom they have pierced, and I gradually come to know what it means to be part of your body and your blood, what it means to be human.

> —*Heart Speaks to Heart*

Lord Jesus, you always call me closer to your wounded heart. There you want me to know true joy and true peace. Gradually I realize that in your heart, seeing and not seeing, hearing and not hearing, touching and not touching are not contradictions. To Thomas who heard your voice, saw your wounds, and touched your pierced side, you said, "You believe because you can see me. Blessed are those who have not seen and yet believe." There, O dear Lord, is the mystery of your love. I have not seen you and yet I truly see you every time I look at the broken bodies of my fellow human beings. I have not heard you, and yet I truly hear the cries uttered by men, women and children in pain. I have not touched you, and yet I truly touch you every time I touch all those who come to me in their loneliness. In the midst of all the human brokenness and human pain, I see, hear, and touch the heart of humanity, your humanity, the humanity of all the people embraced by your love.

Thank you, Jesus, for your heart. Thank you for showing me your heart. Thank you for letting me see while not seeing, hear while not hearing, touch while not touching. Thank you for letting me believe more every day, hope more every day, and love more every day.

My heart is little, fearful, and very timid. It will always be so. But you say, "Come to my heart. My heart is gentle and humble and very broken like yours. Do not be afraid. Come and let your heart find rest in mine and trust that all will be well." I want to come, Jesus, and be with you. Here I am, Lord, take my heart and let it become a heart filled with your love.

—Heart Speaks to Heart

BARNABAS THE APOSTLE
(11 June)

Being a believer means being clothed in Christ. Paul says, "Every one of you that has been baptised has been clothed in Christ" (Galatians 3:27) and "Let your armour be the Lord Jesus Christ"(Romans 13:14). This being "clothed in Christ" is much more than wearing a cloak that covers our misery. It refers to a total transformation that allows us to say with Paul: "I have been crucified with Christ and yet I am alive; yet it is no longer I, but Christ living in me" (Galatians 2:20).

Thus we are the living Christ in the world. Jesus, who is God-made-flesh, continues to reveal himself in our own flesh. Indeed, true salvation is *becoming Christ.*

—*Bread for the Journey*

THE BIRTH OF JOHN THE BAPTIST
(24 June)

Patience dispels clock time and reveals a new time, the time of salvation. It is not the time measured by the abstract, objective units of the clock, the watch, or the calendar, but rather the time lived from within and experienced as full time. It is this full time about which Scripture speaks. All the great events of the Gospels occur in the fullness of time. A literal translation from the Greek shows this clearly: When the time for Elizabeth had *become full* she bore her son John (Luke 1:57). . . .

It is this full time, pregnant with new life, that can be found through the discipline of patience. As long as we are the slaves of the clock and the calendar, our time remains empty and nothing really happens. Thus, we miss the moment of grace and salvation. But when patience prevents us from running from the painful moment in the false hope of finding our treasure elsewhere, we can slowly begin to see that the fullness of time is already here and that salvation is already taking place.

—*Compassion*

PETER AND PAUL, APOSTLES
(29 June)

Each a man of fervent temperament, both found their anger converted into an always-forgiving love.

—*The Genesee Diary*

I have often wondered why these two great apostles are celebrated on the same day. Is not each of them worth a special day?

In his sermon, Pere Thomas responded to this question. He explained how there is always a danger of playing out one against the other: Peter, the simple, uneducated fisherman who had hardly any knowledge of the theological debates of his time and who responded to Jesus in a direct, impulsive way without much distance or criticism; and Paul, the well-educated disciple of Gamaliel, a Pharisee, sharp, intelligent, deeply concerned about the truth, and willing to persecute those whom he considered in grave error. The Church is built on the foundations laid by both Peter and Paul. There are not two churches, one for the simple people who trust their emotions more than their brains and the other for the intellectuals who are willing to debate the current issues. There is only one Church in which Peter and Paul each has his own role and importance. Uncritical Christianity is as dangerous as "pure brain" Christianity. And indeed Paul had deep emotions and Peter engaged in fierce debates. Within the Church there will always be people who romanticize Peter or intellectualize Paul. It is important that both stay together, not only on their feast day, but also in our own way of living a faithful life.

   —*The Road to Daybreak*

. . . After having asked Peter three times if he loved him more than the others and after having commissioned him three times to be a shepherd, he said in a very emphatic way:

> "In all truth I tell you
> When you were young
> you put on your belt
> and walked where you liked;
> but when you grow old
> you will stretch out your hands
> and somebody else will put a belt around you
> and take you where you would rather not go."

   —*(John 21:18)*

These words are the words that made it possible for me to move from Harvard to L'Arche. They touch the core of Christian let go of power and follow the humble way of Jesus. The world says, "When you were young you were dependent and could not go where you wanted, but when you grow old you will be able to make your own decisions, go your own way, and control your own destiny." But Jesus has a different vision of maturity: It is the ability and willingness to be led where you would rather not go. Immediately after Peter has been commissioned to be a leader of his sheep, Jesus confronts him with the hard truth that the servant-leader is the leader who is being led to unknown, undesirable, and painful places. The way of the Christian leader is not the way of upward mobility in which our world has invested so much, but the way of downward mobility ending on the cross. . . . It is not a leadership of power and control, but a leadership of powerlessness and humility in which the suffering servant of God, Jesus Christ, is made manifest.

—*In the Name of Jesus*

THOMAS THE APOSTLE
(3 July)

During a dialogue homily, two of the monks remarked in different ways that although Thomas did not believe in the resurrection of the Lord, he kept faithful to the community of the apostles. In that community the Lord appeared to him and strengthened his faith. I find this a very profound and consoling thought. In times of doubt or unbelief, the community can "carry you along," so to speak; it can even offer on your behalf what you yourself overlook, and can be the context in which you may recognize the Lord again.

John Eudes remarked that Dydimus, the name of Thomas, means "twin," as the Gospel says, and that the fathers had commented that all of us are "two people," a doubting one and a believing one. We need the support and love of our brothers and sisters to prevent our doubting person from becoming dominant and destroying our capacity for belief.

—*The Genesee Diary*

BENEDICT OF NURSIA,
Father of Western Monasticism, c. 550
(11 July)

We are called to a radical break away from ourselves and a total surrender to God. St. Benedict, who so often is praised for his moderation and has even been called a humanist, is no less radical when he speaks about humility, obedience, and having everything in common.

—*The Genesee Diary*

MARY MAGDALENE
(22 July)

Today we heard the story of the encounter between Jesus and Mary of Magdala, two people who love each other. Jesus says, "Mary." She recognizes him and says, "Rabboni," which means "Master" (John 20:16). This simple and deeply moving story brings me in touch with my fear as well as my desire to be known. When Jesus calls Mary by her name, he is doing much more than speaking the word by which everybody knows her, for her name signifies her whole being. Jesus knows Mary of Magdala. He knows her story: her sin and her virtue, her fears and her love, her anguish and her hope. He knows every part of her heart. Nothing in her is hidden from him. He knows her even more deeply and more fully than she knows herself. Therefore, when he utters her name he brings about a profound event. Mary suddenly realizes that the one who truly knows her truly loves her.

I am always wondering if people who know every part of me, including my deepest, most hidden thoughts and feelings, really do love me. Often I am tempted to think that I am loved only as I remain partially unknown. I fear that the love I receive is conditional and then say to myself, "If they really knew me, they would not love me." But when Jesus calls Mary by name he speaks to her entire being. She realizes that the one who knows her most deeply is not moving away from her, but is coming to her offering his unconditional love.

Her response is "Rabboni," "Master." I hear her response as her desire to have Jesus truly be her master, the master of her whole being: her thoughts and feelings, her passion and hope, even her most hidden emotions. I hear her say, "You who know me so fully, come and be my master. I do not want to keep you away from any part of myself. I want you to touch the deepest places of my heart so that I won't belong to anyone but you."

I can see what a healing moment this encounter must have been. Mary feels at once fully known and fully loved. The division between what she feels safe to show and what she does not dare to reveal no longer exists. She is fully seen and she knows that the eyes that see her are the eyes of forgiveness, mercy, love, and unconditional acceptance.

I sense that here, in this simple encounter, we can see a true religious moment. All fear is gone, and all has become love. And how better can this be expressed than by Jesus' words, "go and find my brothers, and tell them: I am ascending to my Father and to your Father, to my God and your God" (John 20:17). There is no longer any difference between Jesus and those whom he loves. They are part of the intimacy that Jesus enjoys with his Father. They belong to the same family. They share the same life in God.

What a joy to be fully known and fully loved at the same time! It is the joy of belonging through Jesus to God and being there, fully safe and fully free.

—*The Road to Daybreak*

JAMES THE APOSTLE
(25 July)

Dear Lord, your disciple James longed for a special place in your reign, a place close to you. You had a special affection for him: you took him with you when you entered the house of Jairus to heal his daughter and when you went up to Mount Tabor to pray. But you made it clear that friendship with you includes suffering with you.

When you asked him if he could drink the cup of suffering, he said yes with the same ambition with which he desired a special place in your reign.

You loved this young, zealous man whose main desire was to be with you at all times and in all places. You told him and all your disciples that service, not power, was the standard in your reign, and slowly you changed his heart from one set on influence into one searching for the deepest place. He responded, followed you, and drank the same cup you drank. He became one of the first apostles to die for you.

O Lord, convert my heart as you converted the heart of your disciple James. Amen.

—*A Cry for Mercy*

IGNATIUS OF LOYOLA,
Founder of the Society of Jesus, 1556
(31 July)

St Ignatius of Loyola was converted by reading the lives of the saints. I can understand this quite well, because every time I read the life of a saint I experience a powerful call to conversion. Every man or woman who lives the Christian life to the full cannot but exercise a deep influence on everyone he or she meets. What continues to fascinate me is that those whose whole mind and heart were directed to God had the greatest impact on other people, while those who tried very hard to be influential were quickly forgotten.

—*¡Gracias!*

Transfiguration

Season of Glory

Transfiguration

Although there is not a season in the Church's year known as "Transfiguration," it seems to have been such an important festival for Henri Nouwen that he reflects on it almost as passionately as he contemplates Holy Week and Easter. Celebrated in the northern hemisphere at the height of summer, the feast day commemorates the occasion when Jesus took Peter, James, and John to the top of a mountain where, in their presence, he was transfigured: his clothes became dazzling white, his face shone like the sun, and a voice disclosed that he was the Beloved. It was a manifestation of divine glory.

The transfiguration took place on Mount Tabor and I was fascinated to learn from Nouwen that, on a visit to the Holy Land, he had once climbed it. But the ever-autonomous pilgrim pointed out that he had not followed the normal route. "I climbed right through the bushes and got totally exhausted, sick, miserable, and lost," he explained. "But when I finally reached the top and looked over, I suddenly saw something I would not have seen if I had taken the bus up. Somehow my whole body was seeing it." He added: "Unless you have climbed the mountain, you cannot appreciate the view."

Transfiguration is an encounter with the sacred which confirms our calling but changes us forever.

I once made my way to the top of a volcanic mountain in the Canary Islands. It wasn't possible to climb too close to the funnel but, even from this vantage point, under the azure sky, the setting was awesome. As I surveyed the panorama and the clouds beneath me, I was suddenly aware both of my dependence on and my closeness to God, an intimacy which filled me with an extraordinary sense of being loved. Later, further down the mountain, in the simple beauty of a silent chapel, in front of a flower-decked altar, I re-offered my life to God. I remember it as an engagement with the divine will, an experience both deeply peaceful and profoundly hopeful.

Transfiguration, then, can be a season in which we celebrate the glorious, transforming power of God and find an isolated place where we can offer ourselves anew. This sequence opens with Henri Nouwen's reflections on the Transfiguration and is followed by thoughts for all those saintly feast days which are celebrated in August, September, and October.

THE TRANSFIGURATION OF THE LORD
(6 August)

When and where do we have an experience of God's Glorious Presence, an experience of unity, an experience of inner fulfilment, an experience of light in the darkness? Peter says: "You do well to be attentive to this as to a lamp shining in a dark place, until the day dawns and the morning star rises in your hearts" (2 Peter 1:19).

Maybe we do not always fully recognize our mountaintop experiences, we write them off as insignificant and trivial compared with all the important and urgent things we have to do. Still, Jesus wants us to see his glory, so that we can cling to that experience in moments of doubt, despair, or anguish. When we are attentive to the light within us and around us, we will gradually see more and more of that light and even become a light for others.

We have to trust that the transfiguration experience is closer to us than we might think. Trusting that, we may also be able to live our Gethsemane experience without losing our faith.

—*Sabbatical Journey*

At some moments we experience complete unity within us and around us. This may happen when we stand on a mountaintop and are captivated by the view. It may happen when we witness the birth of a child or the death of a friend. It may happen when we have an intimate conversation or a family meal. It may happen in church during a service or in a quiet room during prayer. But whenever or however it happens we say to ourselves: "This is it . . . everything fits . . . all I ever hoped for is here."

This is the experience that Peter, James, and John had on the top of Mount Tabor when they saw the aspect of Jesus' face change and his clothing become sparkling white. They wanted that moment to last forever (see Luke 9:28–36). This is the experience of the fullness of time. These moments are given to us so that we can remember them when God seems far away and everything appears empty and useless. These experiences are true moments of grace.

—Bread for the Journey

After the Gospel reading of the transfiguration, the Franciscan climbed the richly carved pulpit in the middle of the cathedral [at Strasbourg]. All the worshippers turned their chairs around so they could see him and listen attentively. He spoke about the transfiguration not only of Jesus, but of all creation. As he spoke he pointed to the brilliant yellow, white, and blue rose window above the cathedral entrance. He said, "Though this is a great piece of art, we can only see its full splendour when the sun shines through it." Then he explained how our bodies, the work of our hands, and all that exists can shine with splendour only when we let God's light shine through them. As he spoke, I kept looking at the magnificent rose window—at thirteen meters across, the largest ever made—and I had a new sense of the transfiguration that took place on Mount Tabor: God's light bursting forth from the body of Jesus. Six centuries ago a rose-window was made that today helps me to see the glory of Christ in a new way.

—The Road to Daybreak

Sensing the touch of God's blessing hands and hearing the voice calling me the Beloved are one and the same. This became clear to the prophet Elijah. Elijah was standing on the mountain to meet God. First there came a hurricane, but God was not in the hurricane. Then there came an earthquake, but God was not in the earthquake. Then followed a fire, but God was not there either. Finally there came something very tender, called by some a soft breeze and by others a small voice. When Elijah sensed this, he covered his face because he knew that God was present. In the tenderness of God, voice was touch and touch was voice.

> —*The Return of the Prodigal Son*

Being the expression of our greatest love, [prayer] does not keep pain away from us. Instead, it makes us suffer more since our love for God is a love for a suffering God and our entering into God's intimacy is an entering into the intimacy where all of human suffering is embraced in divine compassion. To the degree that our prayer has become the prayer of our heart we will love more and suffer more, we will see more light and more darkness, more grace and more sin, more of God and more of humanity. To the degree that we have descended into our heart and reached out to God from there, solitude can speak to solitude, deep to deep and heart to heart. It is there where love and pain are found together.

On two occasions, Jesus invited his closest friends, Peter, John, and James, to share in his most intimate prayer. The first time he took them to the top of Mount Tabor, and there they saw his face shining like the sun and his clothes white as light (Matthew 17:2). The second time he took them to the garden of Gethsemane, and there they saw his face in anguish and his sweat falling to the ground like great drops of blood (Luke 22:44). The prayer of our heart brings us both to Tabor and Gethsemane. When we have seen God in his glory we will also see him in his misery, and when we have felt the ugliness of his humiliation we also will experience the beauty of his transfiguration.

> —*Reaching Out*

The prayer of our heart can grow strong and deep within the boundaries of the community of faith. The community of faith, strengthened in love by our individual prayers, can lift them up as a sign of hope in common praise and thanksgiving. Together we reach out to God beyond our many individual limitations while offering each other the space for our own most personal search. We may be different people with different nationalities, colours, histories, characters and aspirations, but God has called all of us away from the darkness of our illusions into the light of his glory. This common call transforms our world into the place where Gethsemane and Tabor both can exist, our time into the time of patient but joyful waiting for the last day, and ourselves into each other's brothers and sisters.

—*Reaching Out*

. . . *Theologia* is the direct knowledge of God that leads to the contemplation of the Holy Trinity. Here we go beyond the practice of contemplative prayer, and even beyond the vision of the nature of things, and enter into a most intimate communion with God himself. This *theologia* is the greatest gift of all, the grace of complete unity, rest, and peace. It is the highest level of spiritual life, in which the created world is transcended and we experience directly our being lifted up into God's inner life. In this experience, the distinction between ministry and contemplation is no longer necessary since here there are no more blindfolds to remove and all has become seeing.

This *theologia* is the Mount Tabor experience in our lives. It is an experience that is given only to a few, and even they must return to the valley, while being told not to tell others what they have seen. For most of us, the greater part of our life is spent not on the mountaintop but in the valley. And in this valley we are called to be contemplative ministers.

—*Clowning in Rome*

LAWRENCE, Deacon and Martyr, 258
(10 August)

The Church will always be renewed when our attention shifts from ourselves to those who need our care. The blessing of Jesus always comes to us through the poor. The most remarkable experience of those who work with the poor is that, in the end, the poor give more than they receive.

—*Bread for the Journey*

THE ASSUMPTION OF THE BLESSED VIRGIN MARY
(15 August)

The Magnificat speaks about "lifting up the lowly." Mary was lifted up, and not only Mary but all of us who claim for ourselves our true spiritual identity. As people raised up by God's immense grace, all generations will call us blessed.

—*Sabbatical Journey*

. . . Mary is for the monks the most pure contemplative. Luke describes her as contemplating the mysteries of the redemption. After telling about the visit of the shepherds to the Child, he writes: "As for Mary, she treasured all these things in her heart" (Luke 2:19), and after describing how she found Jesus in the temple among the doctors of law, he adds: "His mother stored up all these things in her heart." She is the contemplative of whom the aged Simeon says that a sword will pierce her soul (Luke 2:35).

The doctrine of her Assumption affirms the fulfilment of this contemplative life in heaven. There the most redeemed human being, the woman in whom God touched us in the most intimate way, the mother of Jesus and all who believe in him—there she stands in the presence of God, enjoying forever the beatific vision that is the hope of all monks and all Christians.

—*The Genesee Diary*

BERNARD, Abbot of Clairvaux, 1153
(20 August)

The liturgy was filled with gentle, sometimes sweet, compliments to this great saint of the twelfth century. During the night Office, one of his sermons was read. Simplicity, soberness, and austerity were Bernard's ideals. He practised them too, but his language is wealthy, decorative, ornate, playful, and nearly baroque. His sermons on the Song of Songs belong to the classics of world literature but certainly not because of their sobriety!

—*The Genesee Diary*

BARTHOLOMEW THE APOSTLE
(24 August)

I am struck by the first encounter between Jesus and Bartholomew, who in the Gospel is called Nathanael.

The emphasis is on *seeing*. Jesus said to Nathanael, "Before Philip came to call you, I saw you under the fig tree," and after Nathanael's response: "You are the Son of God," Jesus remarked, "You believe that just because I said I saw you under the fig tree. You will see greater things than that . . . you will see heaven laid open, and above the Son of man, and the angels of God ascending and descending" (John 1:49–51).

The story speaks deeply to me since it raises the questions "Do I want to be seen by Jesus? Do I want to be known by him?" If I do, then a faith can grow which proclaims Jesus as the Son of God. Only such a faith can open my eyes and reveal an open heaven.

Thus, I will see when I am willing to be seen. I will receive new eyes that can see the mysteries of God's own life when I allow God to see me, all of me, even those parts that I myself do not want to see.

O Lord, see me and let me see.

—*The Road to Daybreak*

THE BIRTH OF THE BLESSED VIRGIN MARY
(8 September)

Mary experienced uncertainty and insecurity when she said yes to the angel. She knew what oppression was when she didn't find a hospitable place to give birth to Jesus. She knew the sufferings of the mothers who see their children being thrown in the air and pierced by bayonets; she lived as a refugee in a strange land with a strange language and strange customs; she knew what it means to have a child who does not follow the regular ways of life but creates turmoil wherever he goes; she felt the loneliness of the widow and the agony of seeing her only son being executed. Indeed, Mary is the woman who stands next to all the poor, oppressed, and lonely women of our time. And when she continues to speak to people it is the simple and the poor to whom she appears: Juan Diego, the simple old Mexican Indian of Guadalupe; Bernadette, the poor sickly girl in Lourdes; Lucia, Jacinta, and Francesco, the unspectacular children in Fatima.

Every word in Scripture about Mary points to her intimate connection with all who are forgotten, rejected, despised, and pushed aside. She joyfully proclaims: "He has cast down the mighty from their thrones, and has lifted up the lowly. He has filled the hungry with good things, and the rich he has sent away empty" (Luke 1:52–3). These words today have taken on so much power and strength that, in a country like El Salvador, they are considered subversive and can lead to torture or death. Mary is the mother of the living, the new Eve, the woman who lives deeply in the heart of the Latin American people. She gives hope, inspires the fight for freedom, and challenges us to live with an unconditional trust in God's love.

—*¡Gracias!*

TRIUMPH OF THE CROSS
(14 September)

On the cross, Jesus has shown us how far God's love goes. It's a love which embraces even those who crucified him. When Jesus is hanging nailed to the cross, totally broken and stripped of everything, he still prays for his executioners: "Father, forgive them; they do not know what they are doing." Jesus's love for his enemies knows no bounds. He prays even for those who are putting him to death.

—Letters to Marc about Jesus

OUR LADY OF SORROWS
(15 September)

It takes from 8:30 in the morning until 4:30 in the afternoon to travel from Lourdes to Paris. As I sit in the train, I let the landscape slip by. My thoughts are of Mary, Bernadette, and the ten years ahead of me. The word that comes to mind is "innocent." Mary was innocent. Her soul wasn't wounded by sin. That is why she could offer a perfect place to the child of God. Her innocence was an innocence from which the Word of God could take flesh and become the lamb to take away the sin of the world. Her innocence made her become the Mother of Sorrows because she who had no sin sensed more deeply the sins of humanity for which her son came to suffer and die.

—Jesus and Mary

MATTHEW, Apostle and Evangelist
Death of Henri J.M. Nouwen, 1996
(21 September)

Whatever we do in the Name of Jesus, we must always keep the peace of Jesus in our hearts. When Jesus sends his disciples out to preach the Gospel, he says: "Whatever town or village you go into, seek out someone worthy and stay with him until you leave. As you enter his house, salute it, and if the house deserves it, may your peace come upon it; if it does not, may your peace come back to you" (Matthew 10:11–13).

The great temptation is to let people take our peace away. This happens whenever we become angry, hostile, bitter, spiteful,

manipulative, or vengeful when others do not respond favorably to
the good news we bring them.

—*Bread for the Journey*

Death often happens suddenly. A car accident, a plane crash, a
fatal fight, a war, a flood, and so on. When we feel healthy and full
of energy, we do not think much about our deaths. Still, death
might come very unexpectedly.

How can we be prepared to die? By not having any unfinished
relational business. The question is: Have I forgiven those who
have hurt me and asked forgiveness from those I have hurt? When
I feel at peace with all the people who are part of my life, my death
might cause great grief, but it will not cause guilt or anger.

When we are ready to die at any moment, we are also ready to
live at any moment.

—*Bread for the Journey*

MICHAEL AND ALL ANGELS
(29 September)

I am beginning now to see how radically the character of my spiritual journey will change when I no longer think of God as hiding
out and making it as difficult as possible for me to find him, but,
instead, as the one who is looking for me while I am doing the
hiding. When I look through God's eyes at my lost self and discover God's joy at my coming home, then my life may become less
anguished and more trusting.

Wouldn't it be good to increase God's joy by letting God find me
and carry me home and celebrate my return with the angels?
Wouldn't it be wonderful to make God smile by giving God the
chance to find me and love me lavishly? Questions like these raise
a real issue: that of my own self-concept. Can I accept that I am
worth looking for? Do I believe that there is a real desire in God to
simply be with me?

—*The Return of the Prodigal Son*

FRANCIS OF ASSISI, Founder of the Friars Minor, 1226
(4 October)

. . . A day that needs my special attention since I will need a lot of guidance to find an answer to the question, "What place does poverty really have in my life?" From a statistical point of view, I belong to the few very wealthy people of this world. I earn more money than I need. I have enough to eat, good clothes, a pleasant place to stay, and I am surrounded by family and friends who are willing to help when I have any problems.

Still, without a certain attempt to live a life of poverty I can never call myself a sincere Christian. . . . Three aspects of poverty remain attractive to me: first, living a simple and sober life; second, not trying to be different from my colleagues in externals; and third, spending a good deal of time working with the poor and giving as much money as possible to people who are working to alleviate poverty. I hope St. Francis will help me to discover how to make this concrete.

G. K. Chesterton writes in his book, *St. Francis of Assisi*, that St. Francis's argument for poverty was "that the dedicated man might go anywhere among any kind of men, even the worst kind of men, so long as there was nothing by which they could hold him. If he had any ties or needs like ordinary men, he would become like ordinary men."

. . . Chesterton gives a beautiful insight into the conversion of St. Francis by describing him as the "tumbler for God" who stands on his head for the pleasure of God. By seeing the world upside down "with all the trees and towers hanging head downwards," Francis discovers its dependent nature. The word dependence means hanging. By seeing his world, his city, upside down, Francis saw the same world and the same city but in a different way. "Instead of being merely proud of his strong city because it could not be moved, he would be thankful to God Almighty that it had not been dropped."

This conversion, this turn around, this new view made it possible for Francis to make praise and thanksgiving his central attitude in a world that he had rediscovered in its most profound dependence on God.

Here, indeed, we reach that mysterious point where asceticism and joy touch each other. Francis, who was a very severe ascetic, is, nevertheless, known as the most joyful of saints. His joy about all that is created was born out of his full realization of its dependence on God. In fasting and poverty, he reminded himself and others of God's lordship. In his songs of praise and thanksgiving, he revealed the beauty of all that is obedient to its Creator.

> —*The Genesee Diary*

LUKE the Evangelist, patron of painters
(18 October)

Everyone who touched Jesus and everyone whom Jesus touched were healed. God's love and power went out from him (see Luke 6:19). When a friend touches us with free, nonpossessive love, it is God's incarnate love that touches us and God's power that heals us.

> —*Bread for the Journey*

SIMON AND JUDE, Apostles
(28 October)

The knowledge of being loved in an unconditional way, before the world presents us with its conditions, cannot come from books, lectures, television programs or workshops. This spiritual knowledge comes from people who witness to God's love for us through their words and deeds. These people can be close to us but they can also live far away or may even have lived long ago. Their witness announces the truth of God's love and calls us to act in accordance with it.

> —*Bread for the Journey*

Recollection

Season of Remembrance

Recollection

The death of my father in the prime of his life was naturally distressing. He had brought joy and kindness into the lives of many, not least his own family and the students he taught. We buried his ashes in the family grave but his spirit lived on among us. A few years later I was introduced to the writings of Henri Nouwen. I am certain they helped to heal a deeper degree of separation.

What I found especially poignant and helpful were Nouwen's words on loneliness and death. I was also impressed by his account of Latin American families picnicking on the graves of their ancestors on All Souls' Day. It is reproduced among the following extracts. The grave is a special in-between place, where sacred and linear time meet. I discover at my father's resting place something of the peace I sensed in that mountainside church beneath the volcano.

At the turn of the millennium, inspired by Nouwen, I devised a small liturgy, which I went on to enact in the cemetery. After dusk on New Year's Eve, 1999, I headed out to the grave, lit a candle, and said prayers. It was dark, cold, and silent. The flame held its own against the occasional thrust of wind. Then, encasing the flickering candle with my hands, I walked slowly through the streets as an act of witness. Passing strangers I feared might smirk and mock simply waved and smiled. The pilgrimage was one of

171

extraordinary unity and peace, an act of gratitude that seemed not only to connect the living and the dead but to bridge two millennia in a simple ceremony of mystery and communion.

November is a season of sobriety when we remember those who have gone before us and summon the courage to befriend our own death.

In *Our Greatest Gift*, Henri Nouwen helps us face our own fears of ultimate loneliness and abandonment. Death is an event that separates us from others. It is about departing and the ending of precious relationships. But, as Nouwen reassuringly points out, Jesus died so that our own death need no longer be merely separation. The death of Christ opened for us the possibility of making our own death a way to union and reintegration. Nouwen also reminds us that our lives will continue to bear fruit after we have died. Our spirit will live on in those we love.

I treasure my small hardback edition of this book. The inscription reads: "For Michael Ford: Grateful for your friendship and for your willingness to let me be part of your adventurous journey with God. Love Henri Nouwen."

His influence has been immeasurable, giving me also the confidence to lead my spiritual life with a certain independence and autonomy, pitching my tent on the margins and staying close to an in-between God. The writings of Nouwen are tailor-made for nomads.

The final stage of our liturgical pilgrimage brings us, then, to a season when we acclaim the saints, honour the dead, and reflect on the kingdom in the spirit of the Beatitudes. I remember Nouwen explaining that his experience of living among the developmentally disabled at L'Arche had enabled him to understand the need to live the Beatitudes as fully as possible: "Blessed are the poor. . . . Blessed are those who mourn. . . . Blessed are the peacemakers. . . . " were his three examples. Nouwen keeps the eternal seasons in focus by reminding us that our hope lies not in earthly securities, but in God. Our completion can happen only when we are ready to receive fully the divine life. "God's will is the way God loves us," he told me. "That's what God's will is about."

ALL SAINTS' DAY
(1 November)

Through baptism we become part of a family much larger than our biological family. It is a family of people "set apart" by God to be light in the darkness. These set-apart people are called saints. Although we tend to think about saints as holy and pious, and picture them with halos above their heads and ecstatic gazes, true saints are much more accessible. They are men and women like us, who live ordinary lives and struggle with ordinary problems. What makes them saints is their clear and unwavering focus on God and God's people. Some of their lives may look quite different, but most of their lives are remarkably similar to our own.

The saints are our brothers and sisters, calling us to become like them.

—*Bread for the Journey*

The readings, mostly from the Apocalypse, gave a glorious picture of the New Jerusalem. A city with splendid gates, full of beauty and majesty. We heard about the throne of God and the twenty-four thrones of the elders dressed in white robes with golden crowns on their heads. "Flashes of lightning were coming from the throne, and the sound of peals of thunder, and in front of the throne there were seven flaming lamps burning, the seven Spirits of God" (Revelation 4:5).

The whole day was full of glorious visions, glorious sounds, and glorious spectacles, and it became clear that in this way we were presented with an image of the world to come.

During the day, however, I also read "The Week in Review" of *The New York Times* and was overwhelmed by the misery of this world. More and more it seems that dark clouds are gathering above our world: Asia, Africa, Latin America, Europe, the United States—all over the globe it seems that people are worrying about the dark forces that lead to hunger, war, violence, poverty, captivity and wonder if there is anyone who has the vision and the power that can offer hope for a better future.

I was deeply struck by these contrasting panoramas. How do they relate to each other? Where do they intersect and connect? The Church does not seem to be able to give much of a foretaste of the heavenly glory.

It seems that the vision of All Saints' Day remains "up in the sky," and that even sincere attempts to make it come closer by concrete changes in our present darkness are not very successful. All this made All Saints' Day a somewhat ambiguous feast.

—*The Genesee Diary*

You have to trust that every true friendship has no end, that a communion of saints exists among all those, living and dead, who have truly loved God and one another. You know from experience how real this is. Those you have loved deeply and who have died live on in you, not just as memories but as real presences.

—*The Inner Voice of Love*

Jesus makes it clear that the way to God is the same as the way to a new childhood. "Unless you turn and become like little children you will never enter the Kingdom of Heaven." Jesus does not ask me to remain a child but to become one. Becoming a child is living toward a second innocence: not the innocence of the newborn infant, but the innocence that is reached through conscious choices.

How can those who have come to this second childhood, this second innocence, be described? Jesus does this very clearly in the Beatitudes. Shortly after hearing the voice calling him the Beloved, and soon after rejecting Satan's voice daring him to prove to the world that he is worth being loved, he begins his public ministry. One of his first steps is to call disciples to follow him and share in his ministry. Then Jesus goes up onto the mountain, gathers his disciples around him, and says: "How blessed are the poor, the

gentle, those who mourn, those who hunger and thirst for uprightness, the merciful, the pure of heart, the peacemakers, and those
who are persecuted in the cause of uprightness."

These words present a portrait of the child of God. It is a self-
portrait of Jesus, the Beloved Son. It is also a portrait of me as I
must be. The Beatitudes offer me the simplest route for the journey home, back into the house of my Father. And along this route
I will discover the joys of the second childhood: comfort, mercy,
and an ever clearer vision of God. And as I reach home and feel
the embrace of my Father, I will realize that not only heaven will
be mine to claim, but that the earth as well will become my inher-
itance, a place where I can live in freedom without obsessions and
compulsions.

Becoming a child is living the Beatitudes and so finding the
narrow gate into the Kingdom.

—*The Return of the Prodigal Son*

From God's perspective, one hidden act of repentance, one little
gesture of selfless love, one moment of true forgiveness is all that is
needed to bring God from his throne to run to his returning son
and to fill the heavens with sounds of divine joy.

If that is God's way, then I am challenged to let go of all the
voices of doom and damnation that drag me into depression and
allow the 'small' joys to reveal the truth about the world I live in.
When Jesus speaks about the world, he is very realistic. He speaks
about wars and revolutions, earthquakes, plagues and famines,
persecution and imprisonment, betrayal, hatred, and assassina-
tions. There is no suggestion at all that these signs of the world's
darkness will ever be absent. But still, God's joy can be ours in the
midst of it all. It is the joy of belonging to the household of God
whose love is stronger than death and who empowers us to be in
the world while already belonging to the kingdom of joy.

This is the secret of the joy of the saints. From St. Anthony of
the desert, to St. Francis of Assisi, to Frère Roger Schultz of Taizé,

to Mother Teresa of Calcutta, joy has been the mark of the people of God. That joy can be seen on the faces of the many simple, poor, and often suffering people who live today among great economic and social upheaval, but who can already hear the music and the dance in the Father's house. I, myself, see this joy every day in the faces of the mentally handicapped people of my community. All these holy men and women, whether they lived long ago or belong to our own time, can recognize the many small returns that take place every day and rejoice with the Father. They have somehow pierced the meaning of true joy.

—*The Return of the Prodigal Son*

We often limit the Church to the organisation of people who identify themselves clearly as its members. But the Church as all people belonging to Christ, as that body of witnesses who reveal the living Christ, reaches far beyond the boundaries of any human institution. As Jesus himself said: The Spirit "blows where it pleases" (John 3:8). The Spirit of Jesus can touch hearts wherever it wants; it is not restrained by any human limits.

There is a communion of saints witnessing to the risen Christ that reaches to the far ends of the world and even farther. It embraces people from long ago and far away. It is that immense community of men and women who through words and deeds have proclaimed and are proclaiming the Lordship of Jesus.

—*Bread for the Journey*

ALL SOULS' DAY
(2 November)

Throughout Latin America, All Souls' Day is a special feast. The day in which people pay tribute to and enter into communion with those who have died. The place where this celebration of the lasting bonds with the dead can be experienced is the cemetery.

. . . At 2:30 p.m. I was free to join some friends for a visit to the cemetery of Cochabamba. What I saw there I will never forget.

Thousands of people were sitting and walking around the graves as though they were camping with their beloved ones who had died. All types of sounds were mingled together: the sound of boys praying aloud, the sound of a trumpet, the sound of friendly conversations, the sounds of laughter and tears. Was this a gigantic picnic, a massive wake, a city-wide prayer service, a feast, a reunion, a day of repentance, or a celebration of continuing brotherhood and sisterhood? It obviously was all of that and much, much more. Something became visible at that cemetery that defied our usual distinctions between sorrow and joy, mourning and feasting, eating and fasting, praying and playing, and, most of all, living and dying. The people who came together in the cemetery revealed a reality that cannot be grasped by any of the categories that we use to define our daily experiences.

. . . Wherever we walked people looked at us with friendly smiles, as if they were grateful that we had come. They appeared to be at a party. Each grave was surrounded by people who had spread a blanket over the grave and covered it with food: bananas, oranges, and all forms of *urpo*, a special bread baked for the day. Often the centrepiece was a cake in the form of a man or woman, representing the one who was buried under the blanket. At one place I saw a large bread, standing up in the form of a man with uniform and gun, indicating that the family was mourning the death of a soldier. Sister Jeri explained: "The people bring all sorts of food to the graves, often the food their deceased relatives most liked, and then they have a meal with them and thus continue to stay in touch."

What caught my attention most of all were the praying boys. In pairs, ten-to-twelve year-old boys walked all over the cemetery with large white sacks over their shoulders. One of each couple had a small booklet. They went from grave to grave asking if the people would let them pray. When the answer was yes, they knelt down in front of the grave, one boy loudly reciting the litany printed in his booklet, the other responding even more loudly every ten seconds: "Let us praise the Lord in the Blessed Sacrament of the altar and the Virgin Mary conceived without original sin." It was clear that the boys had hardly any idea what they were saying, but their eyes were tightly closed and their hands devoutly folded. All over the cemetery the boys' voices sounded in a strangely pleasant rhythm that seemed to unite all that was happening into one great prayer.

—*¡Gracias!*

There are many sick people who don't have much understanding of their sickness, and often they die without ever having given much thought to their death. About a year ago a friend of mine died of cancer. Six months before his death, it was already obvious that he hadn't long to live. Even so, it was very difficult to prepare him properly for his death. He was so hedged around with tubes and hoses and busy nurses, that one got the impression that he had to be kept alive at any price. I am not saying that anyone did anything wrong, but I do say that so much attention was given to keeping him alive that there was hardly time to prepare him for death.

The result of this for us is that we no longer pay much attention to the dead. We do little to remember them, that is, to make them a part of our interior life. How often do you visit your grandmother's grave? How often do your mother and I visit the graves of our deceased grandparents, uncles, aunts, and friends? In fact, we behave as though they no longer belong to us, as though we have nothing more to do with them. They no longer have any real influence on our lives. Not only have they gone from us physically, but they have also left the world of our thoughts and feelings.

Jesus' attitude to suffering and death was quite different. For him, they were realities he encountered with his eyes wide open. Actually, his whole life was a conscious preparation for them. Jesus doesn't commend suffering and death as desirable things; but he does speak of them as something we ought not to repudiate, avoid, or cover up. . . .

Living spiritually is made possible only through a direct, uncushioned confrontation with the reality of death.

—*Letters to Marc about Jesus*

BITTER GRIEF

I looked at Adam's casket deep in the grave with one simple bouquet of flowers on top of it, and I knew without a doubt that Adam would never be with us again. Loads of soil would cover his body, and gradually it would become part of the earth surrounding it. It was in front of that big hole that I was confronted with the finality of death as well as with hope in the resurrection.

We all felt it. We dropped the frozen clumps of earth into the grave, and heard the dull noise on the casket, our grieving hearts torn. Michael started to sob in the arms of his friends, and John, finally able to let his sorrow be known, erupted in loud howls of grief. At that moment we knew the depth of our powerlessness and loneliness. The sun, the snow, the bitter cold, the grave, the crying, and Adam's body down in the ground—they told us about our unspeakable sorrow. When we all had our turn with the shovels, we sang again the Irish blessing we had sung in the church, and I said, "Let's now go in peace." Slowly the crowd turned and began to depart.

—Adam

THE ETERNAL NOW

Eternal life. Where is it? When is it? For a long time I have thought about eternal life as a life after all my birthdays have run out. For most of my years I have spoken about the eternal life as the "afterlife," as "life after death." But the older I become, the less interest my 'afterlife' holds for me. Worrying not only about tomorrow, next year, and the next decade, but even about the next life seems a false preoccupation. Wondering how things will be for me after I die seems, for the most part, a distraction. When my clear goal is the eternal life, that life must be reachable right now, where I am, because eternal life is life in and with God, and God is where I am here and now.

The great mystery of the spiritual life—the life in God—is that we don't have to wait for it as something that will happen later. Jesus says: "Dwell in me as I dwell in you." It is this divine indwelling that is eternal life. It is the active presence of God at the

center of my living—the movement of God's Spirit within us—
that gives us the eternal life.

But still, what about life after death? When we live in communion with God, when we belong to God's own household, there is
no longer any "before" or "after." Death is no longer the dividing
line. Death has lost its power over those who belong to God,
because God is the God of the living, not of the dead. Once we
have tasted the joy and peace that come from being embraced by
God's love, we know that all is well and will be well. "Don't be
afraid," Jesus says. "I have overcome the powers of death . . . come
and dwell with me and know that where I am your God is."

When eternal life is our clear goal it is not a distant goal. It is a
goal that can be reached in the present moment. When our heart
understands this divine truth, we are living the spiritual life.

—*Here and Now*

HOMECOMING

Our life is a short opportunity to say "yes" to God's love. Our
death is a full coming home to that love. Do we desire to come
home? It seems that most of our efforts are aimed at delaying this
homecoming as long as possible.

Writing to the Christians at Philippi, the apostle Paul shows a
radically different attitude. He says: "I want to be gone and be with
Christ, and this is by far the stronger desire—and yet for your sake
to stay alive in this body is a more urgent need." Paul's deepest
desire is to be completely united with God through Christ and that
desire makes him look at death as a "positive gain." His other
desire, however, is to stay alive in the body and fulfill his mission.
That will offer him an opportunity for fruitful work.

We are challenged once again to look at our lives from above.
When, indeed, Jesus came to offer us full communion with God, by
making us partakers of his death and resurrection, what else can

we desire but to leave our mortal bodies and so reach the final goal of our existence? The only reason for staying in this valley of tears can be to continue the mission of Jesus who has sent us into the world as his father sent him into the world. Looking from above, life is a short, often painful mission, full of occasions to do fruitful work for God's kingdom, and death is the open door that leads us into the hall of celebration where the king himself will serve us.

It all seems such an upside-down way of being! But it's the way of Jesus and the way for us to follow. There is nothing morbid about it. On the contrary, it's a joyful vision of life and death. As long as we are in the body, let us care well for our bodies so that we can bring the joy and peace of God's kingdom to those we meet on our journey. But when the time has come for our dying and death let us rejoice that we can go home and be united with the One who calls us the beloved.

> —*Here and Now*

THE BEAUTY OF AUTUMN

The autumn leaves can dazzle us with their magnificent colors: deep red, purple, yellow, gold, bronze, in countless variations and combinations. Then, shortly after having shown their unspeakable beauty, they fall to the ground and die. The barren trees remind us that winter is near. Likewise, the autumn of life has the potential to be very colourful: wisdom, humour, care, patience, and joy may bloom splendidly just before we die.

As we look at the barren trees and remember those who have died, let us be grateful for the beauty we saw in them and wait hopefully for a new spring.

> —*Bread for the Journey*

LOVE-BEARING FRUIT

Hope and faith will both come to an end when we die. But love will remain. Love is eternal. Love comes from God and will return to God. When we die, we will lose everything that life gave us except love. The love with which we lived our lives is the life of God within us. It is the divine, indestructible core of our being. This love not only will remain but also will bear fruit from generation to generation.

When we approach death let us say to those we leave behind, "Don't let your heart be troubled. The love of God that dwells in my heart will come to you and offer you consolation and comfort."

—*Bread for the Journey*

RE-MEMBERING

When we lose a dear friend, someone we have loved deeply, we are left with a grief that can paralyse us emotionally for a long time. People we love become part of us. Our thinking, feeling, and acting are codetermined by them. Our fathers, our mothers, our husbands, our wives, our lovers, our children, our friends . . . they are all living in our hearts. When they die a part of us dies too. That is what grief is about: it is that slow and painful departure of someone who has become an intimate part of us. When Christmas, New Year, a birthday, or an anniversary comes, we feel deeply the absence of our beloved companion. We sometimes have to live a whole year or more before our hearts have fully said good-bye and the pain of our grief recedes. But as we let go of them they become part of our "members" and as we "re-member" them, they become guides on our spiritual journey.

—*Bread for the Journey*

GLIMPSING NEW LIFE

My heart refuses to believe that all Adam lived in his body was for nothing. His incredible vulnerability and life, which became the mysterious gateway through which he poured out his love to so many people, are destined for glory. Just as the wounds of Jesus in his risen body were the signs that allowed others to recognize him, Adam's wounds become marks of his unique presence in our midst. Adam's broken body was the seed of his new, risen life. Paul says,

> Someone may ask: How are dead people raised, and what sort of body do they have when they come? How foolish! What you sow must die before it is given new life; and what you sow is not the body that is to be, but only a bare grain, of wheat I dare say, or some other kind; it is God who gives it the sort of body that he has chosen for it, and for each kind of seed its own kind of body. (1 Corinthians 15:35–8)

Adam's unique body is the seed of his resurrected life. When I saw his youthful beauty in the casket I had a glimpse of this new life. I have to trust the visions and dreams of my friends and the new hope that emerges in the hearts of those I tell about Adam's life. I have to trust in what happens through my own and other people's grief. And as I trust I must believe that I will see that the resurrection of Adam, the beloved son of God, is not only something to wait for but also something that is already happening in the midst of our grief.

—Adam

Feasts of Recollection

THE PRESENTATION OF THE BLESSED VIRGIN MARY
(21 November)

I am discovering in my own life as a priest that without Mary I cannot fully enter into the mystery of Jesus' compassionate love. It is hard to explain why this is so, but I see now, mostly retrospectively, how I used to speak more about Jesus than to him. Most of all, I see now how Jesus had become more an argument for the moral life than the door to the mystical life which is the life in communion with God, Father, Son, and Holy Spirit. Mary calls me back to where I most want to be: to the heart of God which, as you know, is also the heart of the world. She calls me to let the passion of Jesus become my passion and his glory become my glory. She calls me to move beyond the dos and don'ts of the morally correct life into an intimacy with God where I can live the sadness, pain, and anguish of this world while already tasting the gladness, joy, and peace of the glorified Lord.

Mary didn't just call me to that life. She also invites you to that same life. That is why with great urgency I ask you to go to Mary and learn from her how to live in this anguishing world as peace-bringing witnesses of her Son.

—*Jesus and Mary*

ANDREW THE APOSTLE
(30 November)

Jesus says: "If anyone wants to be a follower of mine, let him . . . take up his cross and follow me" (Matthew 16:24). He does not say: "Make a cross" or "Look for a cross." Each of us has a cross to carry. There is no need to make one or look for one. The cross we have is hard enough for us! But are we willing to take it up, to accept it as our cross?

—Bread for the Journey

CHRIST THE KING
(Last Sunday of the Church's Year)

No easy feast day for me since I always have associated this feast with a certain triumphalism in the Church and with a militant spirituality, both of which were so much part of my pre-Vatican II Jesuit formation. It also is the day in which I am always confronted with the problem of authority in the Church because it makes me realize how many people in the Church like to play king in Jesus' name. Finally, it is the day in which I have to deal with my own unresolved struggle with obedience and submission . . . today in the liturgy as well as during my meditation, I started to see and feel that Christ became our King by obedience and humility. His crown is a crown of thorns, his throne is a cross. The soldiers knelt before him saying: "Hail, king of the Jews!" And they spat on him and took the reed and struck him on the head with it" (Matthew 27:30). While he hung on the cross, they said: "If you are the King of the Jews, save yourself." Above him there was an inscription: "This is the king of the Jews" (Luke 23:36–8).

The great mystery of this feast is that we are asked to be obedient to him who was obedient unto the death on the cross, that we are asked to renounce our will for him who prayed to his Father: "Let your will be done, not mine" (Luke 22:43), that we are challenged to suffer humiliation for him who was humiliated for our sake. Christ became King by emptying himself and becoming like us.

—*The Genesee Diary*

On the last Sunday of the liturgical year, Christ is presented to us as the mocked King on the cross as well as the King of the universe. The greatest humiliation and the greatest victory are both shown to us in today's liturgy.

It is important to look at this humiliated and victorious Christ before we start the new liturgical year with the celebration of Advent. All through the year we have to stay close to the humiliation as well as to the victory of Christ, because we are called to live both in our own daily lives. We are small and big, specks in the universe and the glory of God, little fearful people and sons and daughters of the Lord of all creation.

—*Sabbatical Journey*

We have to live the rhythm of the liturgical year as the deepest rhythm of our lives.

—*Timothy Radcliffe OP*

Bibliography

The Works of Henri J.M. Nouwen

Intimacy: Pastoral Psychological Essays, Fides, 1969; Harper & Row, 1981

Creative Ministry: Beyond Professionalism in Teaching, Preaching, Counseling, Organizing and Celebrating, Doubleday, 1971

With Open Hands, Ave Maria Press, 1972, new revised edition, 1995

Thomas Merton: Contemplative Critic, Fides, 1972; Harper & Row, 1981

The Wounded Healer: Ministry in Contemporary Society, Darton, Longman and Todd, new edition, 1994

Aging: Fulfillment of Life, co-authored with Walter Gaffney, Doubleday, 1974

Out of Solitude: Three Meditations on the Christian Life, Ave Maria Press, 1974

Reaching Out: The Three Movements of the Spiritual Life, Fount, new edition, 1996

The Genesee Diary: Report from a Trappist Monastery, Darton, Longman and Todd, new edition, 1995

The Living Reminder: Service and Prayer in Memory of Jesus Christ, Seabury, 1977; Harper & Row, 1983

Clowning in Rome: Reflections on Solitude, Celibacy, Prayer and Contemplation, Doubleday Image, 1979

In Memoriam, Ave Maria Press, 1980

The Way of the Heart: Desert Spirituality and Contemporary Ministry, Darton, Longman and Todd, third edition, 1999

Making All Things New: An Invitation to the Spiritual Life, Harper & Row, 1981

A Cry for Mercy: Prayers from the Genesee, Doubleday, 1981

Compassion: A Reflection on the Christian Life, co-authored with Donald P. McNeill and Douglas A. Morrison, Darton, Longman and Todd, 1982

A Letter of Consolation, Harper & Row, 1982

¡Gracias!: A Latin American Journal, Harper & Row, 1983; Orbis, 1992

Love in a Fearful Land: A Guatemalan Story, Ave Maria Press, 1985

In the House of the Lord: The Journey from Fear to Love, Darton, Longman and Todd, 1986

Behold the Beauty of the Lord: Praying with Icons, Ave Maria Press, 1987

Letters to Marc About Jesus, Darton, Longman and Todd, 1988

The Road to Daybreak: A Spiritual Journey, Darton, Longman and Todd, 1989; memorial edition, 1997

Circles of Love: Daily Readings with Henri J.M. Nouwen, edited by John Garvey, Darton, Longman and Todd, 1988

The Primacy of the Heart: Cuttings from a Journal, edited by Lewy Olfson, St. Benedict Center, 1988

Seeds of Hope: A Henri Nouwen Reader, edited by Robert Durback, Darton, Longman and Todd, 1989, new edition 1998

In the Name of Jesus: Reflections on Christian Leadership, Darton, Longman and Todd, 1989

Heart Speaks to Heart: Three Prayers to Jesus, Ave Maria Press, 1989

Beyond the Mirror: Reflections on Death and Life, Crossroad, 1990

Walk with Jesus: Stations of the Cross, Illustrations by Sr. Helen David, Orbis, 1990

Show Me the Way: Readings for Each Day of Lent, edited by Franz Johna, Darton, Longman and Todd, 1993

The Return of the Prodigal Son: A Story of Homecoming, Darton, Longman and Todd, 1994

Life of the Beloved: Spiritual Living in a Secular World, Hodder & Stoughton, 1993

Jesus and Mary: Finding Our Sacred Center, St. Anthony Messenger Press, 1993

Our Greatest Gift: A Meditation on Dying and Caring, Hodder & Stoughton, 1994

With Burning Hearts: A Meditation on the Eucharistic Life, Geoffrey Chapman, 1994

Here and Now: Living in the Spirit, Darton, Longman and Todd, 1994

Path Series: The Path of Waiting/The Path of Power/The Path of Peace, Darton, Longman and Todd; *The Path of Freedom*, Crossroad, 1995

Ministry and Spirituality: Three Books in One, Continuum, 1996

Can You Drink the Cup? The Challenge of the Spiritual Life, Ave Maria Press, 1996

The Inner Voice of Love: A Journey Through Anguish to Freedom, Darton, Longman and Todd, 1997

Bread for the Journey: Thoughts for Every Day of the Year, Darton, Longman and Todd, 1997

Spiritual Journals: Three Books in One, Continuum, 1997

Adam: God's Beloved, Darton, Longman and Todd, 1997

The Road to Peace: Writings on Peace and Justice, edited by John Dear, Orbis, 1998

Sabbatical Journey, Darton, Longman and Todd, 1998

Other Works

Burnham, Andrew (ed.). *A Manual of Anglo-Catholic Devotion*, Norwich, Canterbury Press, 2001

MacGinty, Gerard, OSB (ed.). *Glenstal Bible Missal*, Brepols Collins, Collins Liturgical Australia, 1984

Roskill, Mark (ed.). *The Letters of Vincent van Gogh*, London, Flamingo, 1983

Ross, Maggie. *Seasons of Death and Life*, HarperSanFrancisco, 1990

   The Fire of Your Life. London, Darton, Longman and Todd Ltd, 1992

Uhde, W. *Van Gogh*, London, Phaidon Press Ltd, 1995

Walther, Ingo F. *Vincent van Gogh*, Cologne, Benedikt Taschen, 1990

Weekday Missal, The, A New Edition, London, HarperCollins Religious, 1992

More Favorites from
Henri J.M. Nouwen ...

Can You Drink The Cup?
ISBN: 0-87793-581-5
112 pages / $10.95

With Open Hands
ISBN: 0-87793-545-9
136 pages / illustrated with 68 photos / $12.95

Out of Solitude
Three Meditations on the Christian Life
ISBN: 0-87793-072-4
64 pages, with photos / $6.95

Behold The Beauty of the Lord
Praying With Icons
ISBN: 0-87793-356-1
80 pages / $12.95

Heart Speaks to Heart
Three Prayers to Jesus
ISBN: 0-87793-388-X
64 pages / $7.95

A Spirituality of Waiting
2-cassette program
ISBN: 0-87793-774-5
1 hr. 24 min. / $12.95

The Lonely Search For God
2-cassette program
ISBN: 0-87793-819-9
2 hrs. 30 min. / $14.95

Keycode: F0T010400000